They Changed the World

People of the Manhattan Project

aj Melnick

They Changed the World

People of the Manhattan Project

aj Melnick
Foreword by Governor Bill Richardson

They Changed the World: People of the Manhattan Project

© 2019 Pajarito Press LLC (revised and updated, second printing). First printing 2006. All rights reserved. No portion of this book may be reproduced in any form or by any means, including electronic storage and retrieval systems, except by explicit, prior written permission of the publisher, except for brief passages excerpted for review and critical purposes.

Printed in the United States of America.

Editor/Publisher, Nancy R. Bartlit
Art Director/Publisher, Mark Rayburn
Book Design, Rayburn Design
Copy Editor, Sandy Blanchard, English Ink

Pajarito Press books may be purchased in quantity for business and educational, or sales promotional use.

Pajarito Press LLC, Box 175, Los Alamos, NM 87544 — Orders, 505/553-5199

Melnick, aj 1931–
    They changed the world : people of the manhattan project / portraits and text by aj Melnick
      p. cm.
    ISBN-13: 978-1-948386-02-9 (hard cover :)

    1. Scientists—New Mexico—Los Alamos—History—20th century—Portraits. 2. Manhattan Project (U.S.)—Biography—Portraits. 3. Los Alamos Scientific Laboratory—Biography—Portraits. 4. United States—Army. 5. World War II—SED—Special Engineer Detachment.
    I. melnick, aj, 1931– II. Title.

On the cover: The Manhattan Project Patch/Insignia. *The background of the [Manhattan Project] patch was blue which represented the universe. A white cloud and lightening bolt form a question mark which symbolizes the unknown results and the secrecy surrounding the project. The lightning bolt extends down to split a yellow atom which represents atomic fission and the expected success of the test. A red and blue star in the center of the question mark is the insignia for the Army Service Forces to which soldiers working on the Manhattan Project were assigned. (Courtesy of White Sands Missile Range)*

Pajarito Press

Pajarito Press LLC – Box 175 – Los Alamos, NM 87544 USA
505/662-5286 • Orders, 505/553-5199 • FAX 505/500-8138
www.pajaritopress.com • info@pajaritopress.com

For my wonderful husband, Harold,
and my three daughters
Susan, Vikki, and Patrice
who cheered me on

Contents

Acknowledgments 9
Speial Comments 10
Foreword by Governor Bill Richardson 11
Prologue 12
Oppenheimer Letter 17
*Aeby, Jack 18
Allred, Elizabeth (Bode) [Singer] 20
*Balagna, John 22
*Boone, Zenas "Slim" 24
*Branson, Esther (Leach) 26
*Bridge, Edulia (Bustos) 28
*Bridge, James "Jim" 30
*Brixner, Berlyn 32
*Caldes Margaret "Beebe" 34
*Caldes, William. "Bill" 36
*Carlson, Bengt 38
*Chavarria, Beatrice (Dasheno) 40
*Chouinard, Consuelo (Meyer) 42
*Cowan, Helen (Dunham) 44
*Cox, Marian (Long) 46
*Dabney, Jean (Waiter) 48
*Davis, Neil 50
*Dike, Margaret 52
*Diven, Benjamin "Ben" 54
*Diven, Rebecca "Beckie" (Bradford) 56
Duran, Charlotte 58
*Fishbine, Hal 60
*Fulgenzi, Consuelo (Connie) 62
Geoffrion, Carmen 64
Gonzales, Severo 66
*Hemmindinger, Arthur (Art) 68
*Hemmindinger, Peggy 70
*Hoogterp, Carlton 72
Hudgins, William (Bill) 74

*Knobeloch, Gordon 76
*Krikorian, Katherine (Pat) 78
*Leary, Joseph A. (Joe) 80
*Mark, Kathleen (Kay) 82
*Martinez, Angelita 84
*Mench, John 86
*Merryman, Roy 88
*Michnovicz, John (Mike) 90
Michnovicz, Mary Lou 92
Moorman, Marian 94
*Moulton, George 96
*Nereson, Jean 98
Norwood, William (Bill) 100
*Osvath, Florence 102
*Osvath, Frank 104
*Prestwood, Rene 106
*Rasmussen, Jane 108
*Rasmussen, Roger 110
*Rosen, Louis 112
Roybal, Julia 114
*Sanchez, Ramon 116
Sandoval, Secundino 118
*Schelberg, Arthur (Art) 120
*Schreiber, (Marguerite) Marge 122
*Sheinberg, Haskell 124
*Snowden, Harry 126
*Stack, Katherine (Katie) 128
*Velasco, Rudolph O. (Rudy) 130
*Walker, Robert (Bob) 132
*Wechsler, Jacob (Jay) 134
*Wilder, Dulcinea (Duddy) 136
Zeltmann, Alfred (Al) 138

* Deceased at the time of printing

Acknowledgments

I am grateful to many people for their assistance, support, and patience. First, of course, are the people of "The Hill" who welcomed me into their homes and searched tirelessly for old photographs and allowed me to use them. Without their cooperation and help, this historical documentary would not have been possible. A special thanks goes to Jean Dabney who provided the copy of her Oppenheimer letter. My husband Harold suffered through my long absences while I was in the darkroom; he both encouraged and helped, never losing faith in me. He is my best editor and critic. Susan, Vikki, and Patrice, my three daughters, gave me wise advice as well as encouragement.

Miguel Gandert, documentary photographer extraordinaire, has been instructor, mentor, and friend; I could not have done this without his continual challenges and encouragement. One could not ask for better friends than Lucian and Joan Niemeyer. Lucian, an exceptional photographer himself, has been my advocate as well as advisor. Joan accompanied and assisted me at many shoots, often entertaining a spouse while I interviewed and photographed. Haskell Sheinberg, a good friend to Harold and me, provided me with a real U.S. Army patch (pictured on the cover) worn by servicemen who worked on the Manhattan Project. Other friends listened tirelessly as I recounted stories I had heard—and were sounding boards for me. I thank them for their enthusiasm as well as their tolerance. Les Sims continually encouraged and supported me. His wife Jan helped me prepare a grant application to the Los Alamos National Bank. And, Hedy Dunn, Director of the Los Alamos Historical Museum, at that time, accepted the portraits for exhibit at the Museum on trust, having seen only the proofs. Thanks, Hedy, for your help and faith in me. I also thank former Governor Bill Richardson for providing the foreword for this book.

Alan Carr, Los Alamos National Lab Senior Historian, and Rebecca Collinsworth, Los Alamos Historical Museum archivist, were terrific; they searched and found some of the old historic photos I needed. And thanks to Marian Cox who went through her photo albums—a historic gold mine for me—where we found photos no one else had. All in all, I feel very lucky and blessed with these special people around me.

Special Comments

*T*he anecdotes in this book have not been changed from the first printing in 2006, but some fact updates have been included. The people portrayed here all worked at the Los Alamos Laboratory (Project "Y"), unless otherwise noted.

―――――

*F*rom 2007 to 2017, framed prints of aj's photo-portraits with the vignettes were displayed on a wall in the Bradbury Science Museum's History Gallery. During this time the Bradbury acquired them and they have become part of the museum's exhibit collections. In 2017, aj's work was incorporated into an interactive display on that same wall, and the physical photo-portraits were reformatted enabling display of a rotating selection. In 2018, aj donated the negatives of the photo-portraits to the Bradbury, and they are now also part of the museum's exhibit collections. The Bradbury Science Museum is part of the Los Alamos National Laboratory located in Los Alamos, New Mexico.

―――――

Following are the comments of Frank Norris after viewing the exhibit mentioned above at the Brabury Science Museum in Los Alamos New Mexico

"*T*he exhibit was Wonderful! Warm, clear, well-presented, really Human. After looking over the many technical displays (regarding the process by which Fat Boy was detonated—which is important, mind you), it was a breath of fresh air to allow these people to tell their stories. I loved the fact that you chose a little of everybody—men and women, different ethnicities, varying ages, a variety of technical and professional roles—and the whole scientific "experiment" makes a lot more sense now. I especially enjoyed the story of the fellow who wanted a machine that pulverized materials ...he needed to ask further questions about it, but couldn't be too open about it for fear of betraying the lab's scientific purpose. I also enjoyed, from several people, telling about the key role that a certain lady played (at 109 E. Palace) in largely coordinating operations—and answering a slew of questions—from the Santa Fe end of things.

So glad I saw it! And thanks so much for all the effort it took to do the research and get the display installed. Very Well Worth It."

—Frank Norris
Historian

Foreword

In the dark days of World War II, the chance event of a prominent scientist having come upon a boys' school years previously while riding horseback in the New Mexico mountains, set in motion a chain of events that ushered in a new era for humanity. Along the way, it led to the creation of a secret city and a secret laboratory on a mountain plateau above Santa Fe—feats of scientific innovation and human ingenuity that would have done credit to an Ian Fleming James Bond novel.

That scientist was J. Robert Oppenheimer, head of the Manhattan Project—the wartime science project that led to the creation of Los Alamos and the development of the atomic bomb. Oppenheimer chose the Pajarito Plateau for his laboratory, and New Mexico became the prime site for this development that changed the direction of human history.

Behind the new reality of nuclear fission, and the sudden existence of the city and the vast laboratory that came to light only after the end of the war, there were people. Not only were there scientists, but also regular people—clerks, truck drivers, teachers—all the skill sets needed to populate Los Alamos, New Mexico.

Santa Fe photographer and writer aj Melnick sought out these people. Through the lens of her camera and the pages of her notebook, she brings to life the realities of living in this quick-built secret city. She has collected the images, both in photographs and in prose, of the lives and times of those people who were every bit as essential to the Manhattan Project as the Oppenheimers and the Tellers.

The members of the early Los Alamos community are a unique fraternity amid the diversity of New Mexico. For New Mexicans and the world at large, Melnick's work revives the experience of living through the creation of a town, a laboratory, and a device that was arguably the most awesome—and most ominous—scientific accomplishment of the 20th Century.

—Bill Richardson, Governor of New Mexico
(Former Secretary of Energy during the administration of President Bill Clinton), 2006

Prologue

Picture in your mind Los Alamos in the early days of World War II, November, 1942: Pajarito Plateau, a mesa in northern New Mexico which had been formed by a lava flow, surrounded by deep canyons and overlooking the Rio Grande. The Jemez Mountains rise to the west, the Sangre de Cristo Mountains to the east. As far as the eye can see, trees cover the spectacular landscape. This was to be the site for Project Y, the most secretive project in which the U.S. had ever been involved.

The U.S. was at war with Germany, Italy, and Japan. The war was not going well. It was known that Germany was working on an atomic bomb; the U.S. needed to develop one first. Preliminary work was in progress in various places in the U.S.; however, the War Department needed a separate facility specifically for research and development of the atomic bomb, in a location that met these essential criteria:

(Photographs on pages 12, 13, and 14 by John "Mike" Michnovicz)

- ✦ A proper site needing that needed a minimum of preparation, so construction of labs and other buildings could begin immediately

- ✦ Existing housing for thirty of the first scientists

- ✦ Land either owned by the government or that could be acquired easily and secretly at a reasonable cost

- ✦ Located far from the sea coasts to minimize possibility of attack

- ✦ Readily-controlled access to the site

- ✦ Existing roads and a nearby railroad to transport materials and personnel

- ✦ An area large enough to accommodate widely-separated testing sites

Other considerations included availability of electric power, water, fuel, construction materials, and local labor. The climate needed to be moderate so that construction could continue during the winter. Because the project was top secret, a remote, sparsely-populated area was sought.

Places which were considered, but eventually eliminated, included the New Mexico locations of Gallup, Las Vegas, La Ventana, and Jemez Springs. Finally, a site that seemed to meet these criteria was found: the Los Alamos Ranch School at Los Alamos, New Mexico. The government already owned most of the surrounding land, 46,000 acres, which was supervised by the U.S. Forest Service. The only additional property to be acquired was the Los Alamos Ranch School itself with its multiple buildings.

J. Robert Oppenheimer, who would later become project director, was consulted about the proposed location. He already knew the area and liked it. He had a summer home in the mountains near Santa Fe, and, during a pack trip several years earlier, had come upon the school. He had been captivated by the view and had visited the school many times. The site selection was made final on November 25, 1942.

The War Department condemned the school; then all records of the transaction were immediately sealed. The school was given until February to finish the academic year and explain to the parents that the school was closing. Of course, the parents were not told the reason. Then, in early 1943, the University of California was selected to operate the Lab.

Major General Leslie R. Groves, as Commanding General, Manhattan Engineer District, Army Service Forces, chose Oppenheimer to be project director of the Lab in spite of concerns from the Military Policy Committee, but the Committee could not offer a better candidate. Several reasons have been given for Groves's choice. Oppenheimer, a theoretical physicist and professor at the University of California at Berkeley, was, according to Groves, "a genius." Also, Oppenheimer was charismatic and charming. It was thought that his scientific stature and his personality would attract other top scientists to the project. And that is what happened.

Oppenheimer gathered together at Los Alamos a "brain trust"—the world's best scientific minds. Once the project was underway, the scientists met with him at the weekly colloquium to report on progress and share information from the different divisions. Five Nobel Prize-winning scientists and one future recipient sat in the front row.

No one worked in isolation; everyone was valuable. This undertaking was a group effort involving all persons, including the janitorial staff. It is said that without Oppenheimer's leadership, the bomb might never have been built.

Opppenheimer's charisma touched everyone on "The Hill," as Los Alamos became known. He was first to comfort a grieving family. He was always the center of attention. He was a gourmet cook who loved to host dinner parties. At a party, his knowledge of diverse subjects was boundless. Women loved him for his attentiveness; he would get down on his knees to talk with a woman who was sitting. After the war, whenever a WAC was discharged, she received a personal letter from him thanking her. (He had consulted with her commanding officer so that he could include the details of her contributions.)

Former WAC Sergeant Jean (Waiter) Dabney wrote that "...[his letter] is one of my special treasures. I wanted to share this with you so you could appreciate what a caring and exceptional man Mr. Oppenheimer was. I'm sure many of the service men and women received this type of letter. Weren't we fortunate to have been stationed there at that time in history—and to be able to assist these great scientists?" (See letter on page 17.)

Among the people working at the Lab, the sense of urgency was pervasive. The United States had a limited amount of time to develop the atomic bomb—before the Germans did. Only those actually involved knew they were working on the bomb. Others knew only that the project had something to do with the war effort and was very important.

Secrecy was a top priority. Those living on The Hill were isolated from the rest of the world. Incoming- and outgoing mail was examined by censors. The return address was P.O. Box 1663, Santa Fe, New Mexico. Some of the men noted even being warned about spies; no one discussed the work outside of the Lab.

The site was surrounded by a high fence topped with three strands of barbed wire. Military Police guarded the premises, and checked security IDs of everyone who went out or came in. MPs patrolled the perimeter on horseback. It was a very safe place. No one needed to worry about children being harmed or lost.

Isolated from the rest of the world, the people on The Hill tried to live normal lives, all the while working toward developing the atomic bomb, an awesome weapon which would end World War II and change life forever. These were a special breed who tolerated the inconveniences of daily living in a make-do atmosphere where the streets were either muddy or dusty and wooden boards served as sidewalks—if there were any sidewalks at all.

Friendships were forged out of common interests, a common goal, a common need. Although 641 women worked in the Lab, most of the workers were men. The lives of the wives were often lonely; the men usually worked long hours, coming home for dinner, then returning to the lab to work well into the night. Therefore, the wives socialized with each other, depended on each other for companionship as well as support. Going to the laundry was a social occasion, with children playing outside as their mothers did the family wash alongside friends.

This was a special time for all who were there. As you look at the faces and read the stories, visualize what their lives might have been like during those war years. Look at the strength and character of the people who were part of the event that forever changed the world.

My talks with the people who were on The Hill (in what is now Los Alamos) during the World War II years of 1943 to 1945 introduced me to a group of interesting people who exhibited a rare, amazingly vibrant spirit. They included technicians, scientists, engineers, housekeepers, wives, WACs, clerks, secretaries, a teacher, young students, photographers, a truck driver.

The project and the people completely captivated and energized me. It became my passion. At the onset, my knowledge of what had transpired at Los Alamos during the war was, at best, sketchy; but the facts I learned and the stories I heard piqued my interest and curiosity.

As I planned, interviewed, and photographed, I became consumed by the quest. I was always looking down the road for the next subject and another original story. I spent the hours driving to and from Albuquerque or Los Alamos or wherever, thinking about what else I could do, whom else I could interview and photograph. I wanted as wide a spectrum of people and their functions as possible, and I worked at making that a reality.

The series evolved from just portraits, to portraits with stories. And then I thought it would be interesting to have photos of the people as they looked during the war. To locate the people, I initially used a Lab retirement list that included retirement dates. I was helped immensely by those who suggested others to interview and photograph, and who sometimes made the initial contact by phone for me.

These are special, human-interest stories that have not been previously recorded. I set out to preserve the stories along with portraits of the people who told them to me. I knew there was an immediacy to the project—these are stories from people who lived and worked at a project that changed the world more than half a century ago— and I was impelled to record their images and their stories.

This documentary series was completed over a period of about two years. The people in this series lived in Los Alamos, Santa Fe, Albuquerque, Española, White Rock, San Ildefonso Pueblo, or Santa Clara Pueblo. I interviewed them in their own homes before I photographed them. (It is necessary for me to establish a bond with each person I photograph to get the best portrait possible.) I usually spent two hours talking with and photographing each subject. I looked for the best location in or around the home for the photographs. For the portraits, I preferred to work in the morning or late afternoon, when the extraordinary New Mexico light is most beautiful.

Most of the photographs were taken in available light using 35 mm cameras—a Canon AE-1 or F-1 with a 50 mm. lens. Film was either Fuji Acros or Ilford Delta, depending on the light. The stories were taken from the interviews and, with one exception, written by me.

—aj Melnick 2006

P. O. BOX 1663
SANTA FE, NEW MEXICO

1 October 1945

M/Sgt. Jean L. Waiter

Dear Miss Waiter:

This letter is to acknowledge your contribution to the development of the atomic bomb. The striking success of this project was made possible only by the work and sacrifices of the Military Personnel.

According to your Group Leader, you are to be especially commended for twenty-six months' service in the work of the laboratory. You spent fifteen months working in electronics where you used your sound, common sense and the technical knowledge in this field with which you came to the laboratory. For the past nine months, you have had a position involving a multitude of duties and responsibilities. These duties ranged from technical work, much of which was new to you, to work equivalent to that of an executive secretary. Your technical knowledge made it possible for you to relieve the senior members of your group of much routine work with which, however, a non-technical secretary would have been unable to cope. All these things you have done cheerfully and well.

Your willingness to work long hours when the work was pressing is to be commended particularly highly because, for much of your time here, you had rather extensive duties in connection with the WAC detachment in addition to your technical duties. Your constant attention to detail, spirit of cooperation with other members of the groups, and your versatility have contributed greatly to the success of the work.

You are encouraged to use this letter as a reference.

Yours very truly,

J. Robert Oppenheimer, Director

Jack Aeby, civilian

- ✦ Worked June, 1943–1975
- ✦ Education: physics and chemistry
- ✦ Technician with Physics Group (which made its own equipment)
- ✦ Worked with the Diagnostic Team checking fission for the yield

George Farwell and Jack Aeby worked at a site in Pajarito Canyon in what was once a U.S. Forest Service area. Several radiation detectors in the area read the levels of various types of radiation. Each day, they went to the area to change the car batteries that powered the detectors.

One day, after they had finished their work, they walked back to their vehicle, an army sedan, only to discover that they had a flat tire. Tires were in short supply in those days and the car had no spare. Since there was almost no traffic on the road, there was nothing for them to do but hike back out, so they began their walk. Suddenly, out of the silence. came a distinct, loud rattle. The guys had come upon a rattlesnake sunning itself directly in their path, and it was not happy about being disturbed.

"I did a big, sideways jump," recalled Aeby. "We had to kill the snake, and we brought it back with us, all six-feet two-inches and ten rattles of it. George kept the rattles."

———

The Pajarito Canyon site had twenty-four-hour Military Police guards. One day the two men came upon an MP asleep at his post, his chair tilted back, his loaded gun leaning against the wall. Leaving the MP undisturbed in his dreams, Farwell and Aeby went about their work which took about an hour. When they returned, the guard was still asleep.

"I took three shells out of his gun and we left. I would have liked to have heard what the MP told his commanding officer. Each shell had to be accounted for," noted Aeby.

———

On another occasion at the Canyon, they found MPs trying to get a bear cub down from a tree. Bears were the symbolic mascots of some of the sports teams on The Hill; the MPs decided they wanted this hundred-pound cub as their live mascot. Finally, they managed to knock the frightened cub to the ground where it lay dazed. The guards then tied a rope loosely around the bear's neck and talked Farwell and Aeby into taking it back for them.

This time Farwell and Aeby had an open command car, two seats in front and two in back. The captive bear was tied in the backseat and off the three went.

Throughout the journey the two men had to duck to elude the bear as it it swiped at them over the seat.

"It was an interesting trip back," reported Aeby. "It was hard to drive and avoid those swinging claws." Eventually the fortunate bear cub gained its freedom because he refused to eat in captivity. Guess he didn't like the menu... ✦

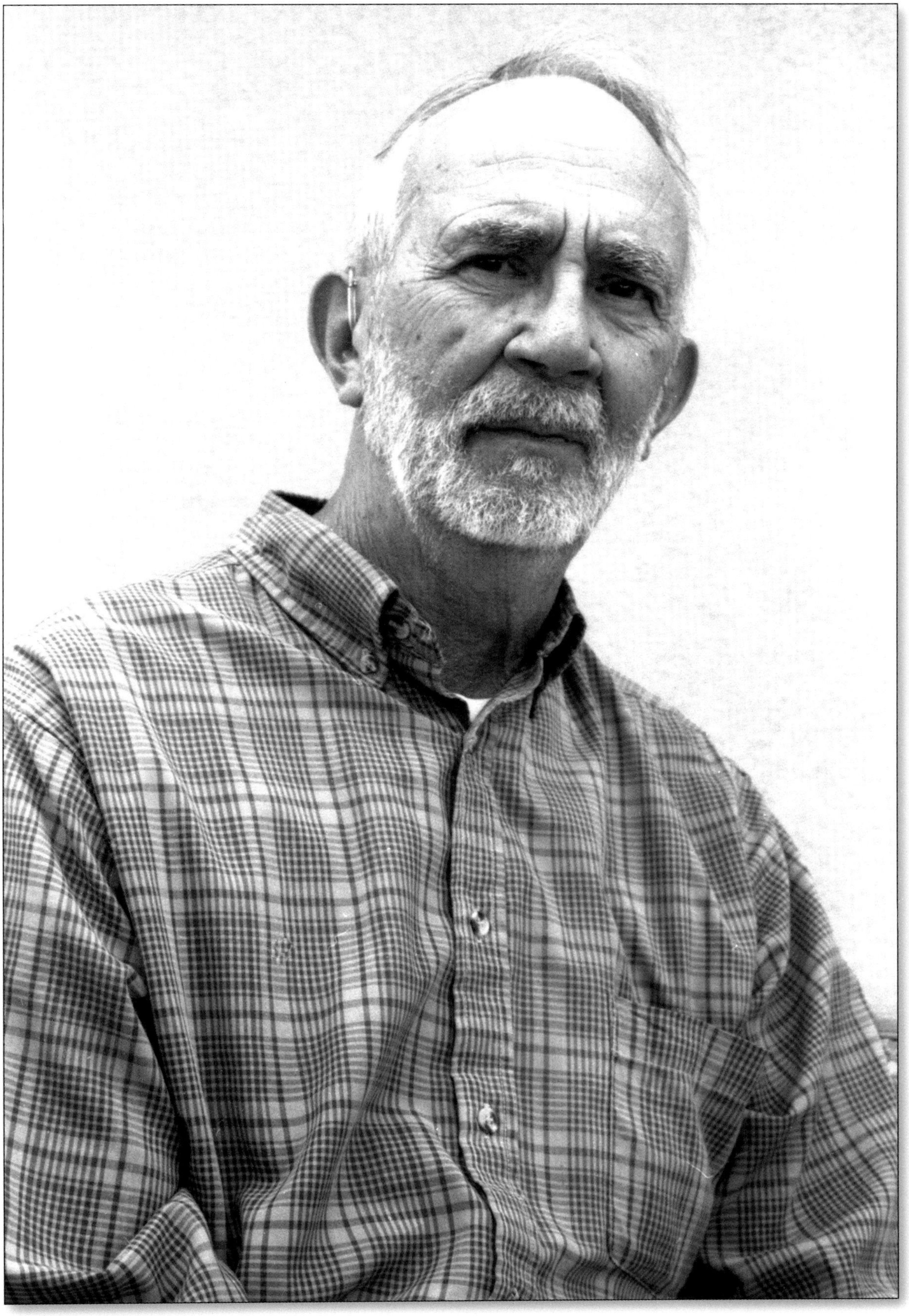

Mary Elizabeth (Bode) [Singer] Allred

- ✦ Worked summers, 1944 and 1945
- ✦ Various jobs: file clerk, waitress at the Mess Hall

What an adventure it was for sixteen-year-old Elizabeth Bode to work and earn money for the first time in her life! She was a junior at Loretto Academy in Santa Fe, but she lived in Abiquiu. Some of her neighbors worked on The Hill and she commuted to work with them. "It was such fun for a country girl," said Allred, "and the military people seemed to have such a good time too."

"I was just a 'gofer' girl the first summer," she related, "and the second summer I got to live in the women's dorm." Bode was the youngest in the dorm, which housed mostly WACs and secretaries, and she had her own room. She liked her dorm mates and shared meals with them. Sometimes they went home with her to Abiquiu to visit. She was very shy in those days, she said, so would have nothing to do with the servicemen.

She remembers one time when she was living in the dorm, one of the women brought in a boyfriend. He had nowhere to stay and hid behind the couch.

"I had a feeling of patriotism and others did too. It was a team effort. I had no idea what was going on, but I knew it was for a good cause. Rumors were abundant, but it was still a mystery to me." ✦

One of the women's barracks *(Courtesy of Los Alamos Historical Society Archives)*

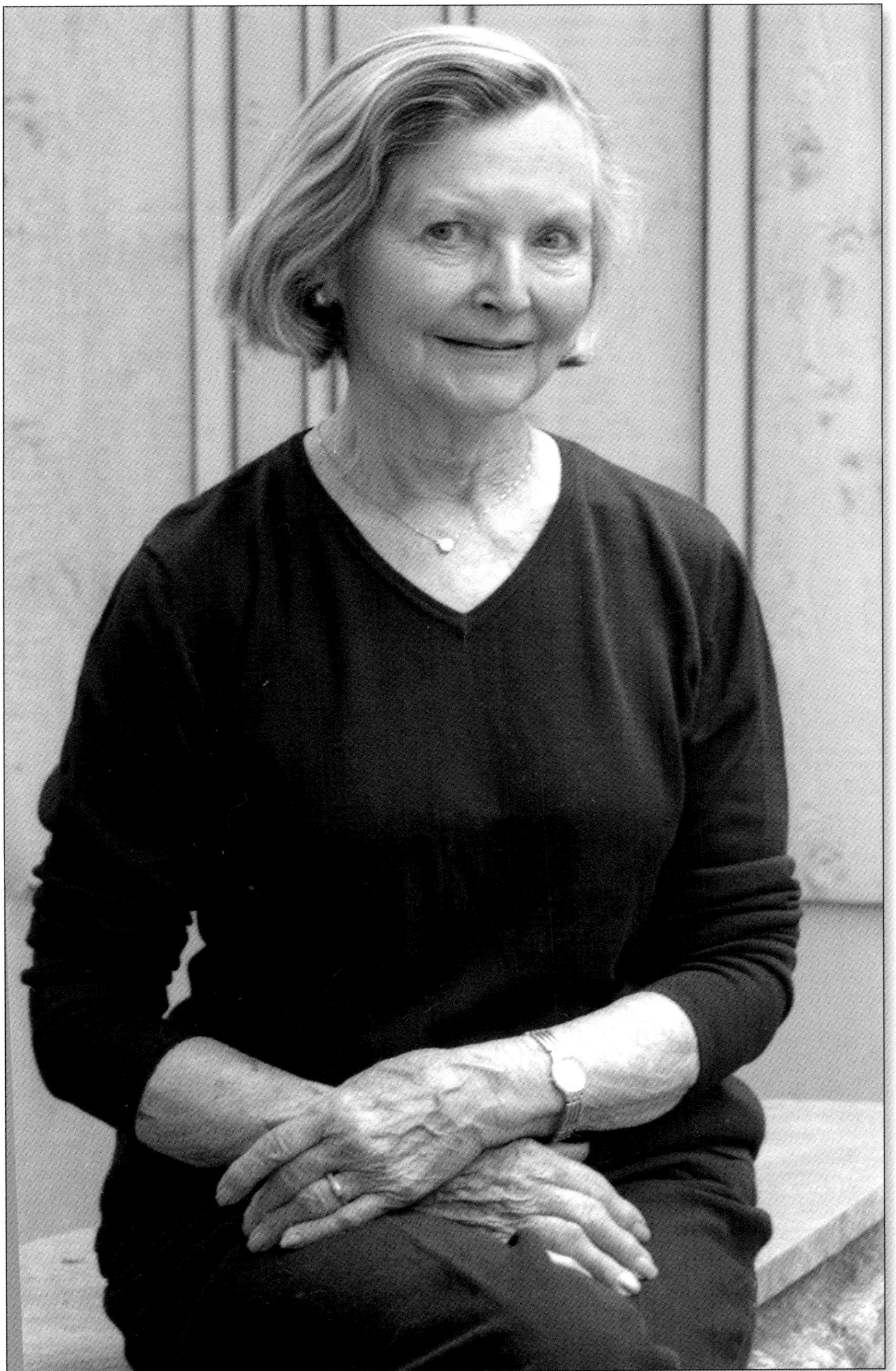

John Balagna, civilian

+ Worked February, 1944–February, 1986
+ Analytical chemist
+ Test Division of atomic bomb

John Balagna was assigned to Dorm 179. On his first night, not having anything else to do, he went down to the day room to check out what was going on. A poker game was in progress, so he introduced himself and joined in. One of the players, John Baudino, said, "I know the name Balagna." Balagna asked Baudino where he was from; Baudino said he was from Peoria, Illinois. The two men then traced their families back to 1820 and came to a startling discovery: their great grandfathers were brothers!

Balagna later learned that Baudino was an agent of the FBI and bodyguard for Enrico Fermi, one of the foremost scientists working on the atom bomb.

(Photos Courtesy of Los Alamos Historical Society Archives)

Dorm 179 was infamous for its wild Saturday night parties. Balagna says that one Saturday night he was in charge of drinks for the party. About 5:30 he began mixing drinks in a new, thirty-gallon garbage can. First he half-filled the can with alcohol from the lab; then filled the rest of the can with orange, grape, and grapefruit juices. To complete the potent brew, he added a block of dry ice so it would smoke.

Of course, when making up such a concoction, you have to taste it to make certain it will be good. And he tasted it often, he related, so much so that by 8 pm he had passed out and was put to bed by his friends.

In the morning, when he awoke, imagine his surprise at finding his bed companion was a WAC named Black Mike, who had passed out early in the evening too. Both were still fully dressed, he noted.

Hmm... We wonder if John's experience in drink-making eventually led him to become a wine maker and entrepreneur. He at one time had a successful business, "Los Santos Wines," in White Rock, New Mexico. ✦

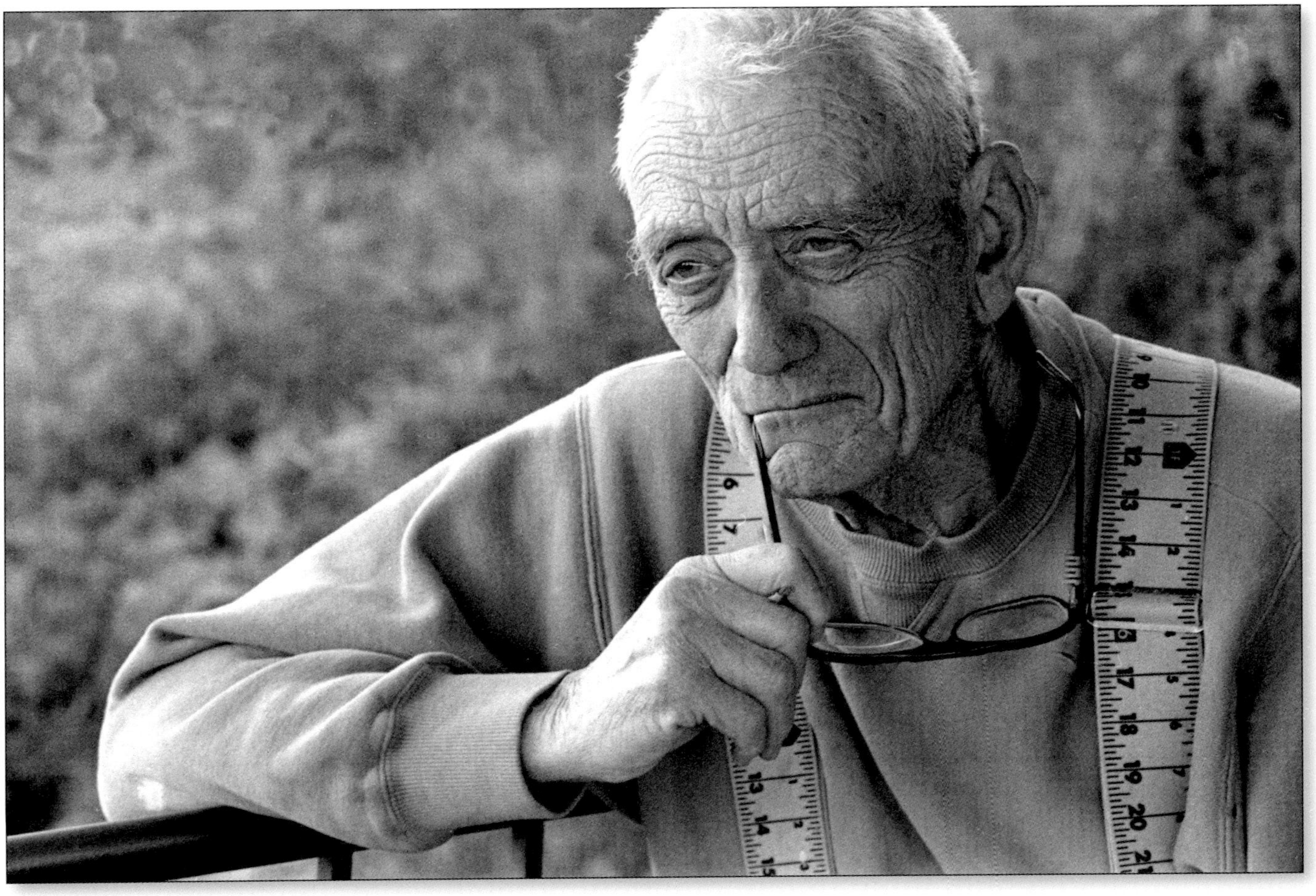

Zenas (Slim) Boone, U.S. Army

✦ (SED) Special Engineer Detachment, June, 1945–1947
✦ Civilian employee 1947–1977
✦ Electronics and explosives

Sixty SEDs came to The Hill from Fort Mead, Maryland. Among them was "Slim" Boone. He was needed on The Hill at the Explosives Division because of his previous experience with explosives. "I wasn't afraid of working with those materials," asserted Boone.

New Mexico was a shock to Boone. "I couldn't believe Santa Fe was the capital of the state; we had county seats back East bigger than Santa Fe. And, I couldn't believe where the troop car was taking this mama's boy!"

He recalled that sometimes it got so cold at Los Alamos that water pipes froze. To avoid having to build fires to thaw the pipes, he would get a pass and take the bus to a hotel in Santa Fe. "That was better than being cold," he said.

Animals were a part of daily life on The Hill. A wolfhound named Timmy did not seem to belong to any one person. Boone said Timmy roamed the area and everyone took care of feeding and petting him. A burro lived at Anchor Ranch near S Site (where explosives were tested). "My buddy had a couple of horses," said Boone, "who seemed to need a lot of exercise. I rode them one July Fourth and didn't often do that again. They made my butt sore," he concluded.

Sometimes, to make a little money, he would help Marian Arnold, whose husband played in the band, collect tickets at the dances. That was an easy five dollars. People would come by and give Arnold a drink of their liquor. "I think they felt sorry for me, so I would be offered a drink too. I had a pretty good time before the dance."

"Oppie (Project Director J. Robert Oppenheimer) was the G.I.s' friend," asserted Boone. "He said we were his boys, and he looked out for 'us' We didn't usually have to stand for inspection and we didn't pull K. P. But the men worked hard, often until midnight, six days a week."

"The army would let you out if you'd stay in the same job at Los Alamos. I was released from the army in 1947 under Section Ten and retired from the Lab in 1977.

"I am proud of being a part of the development of the atom bomb. I am not the least bit ashamed." ✦

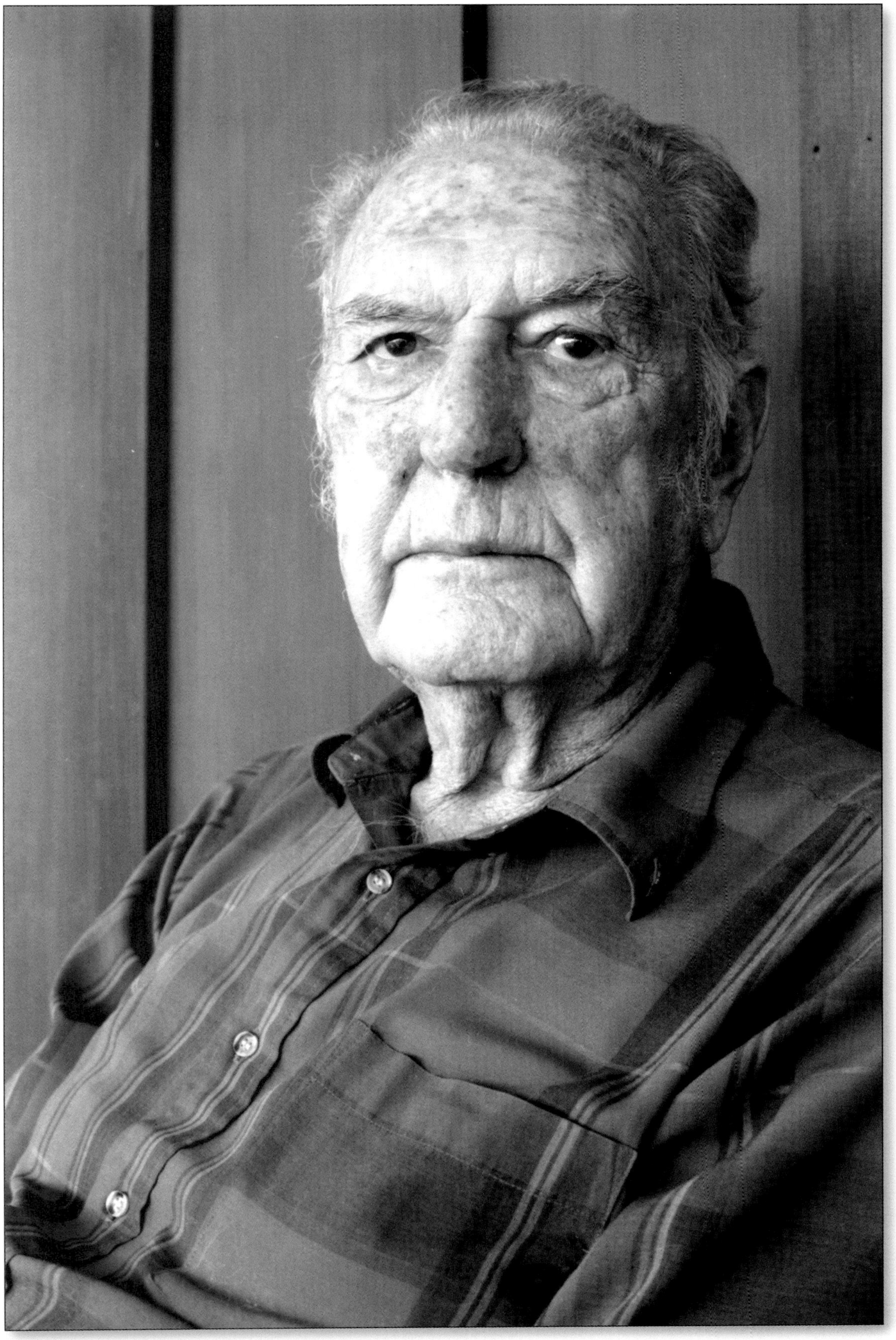

Esther (Leach) Branson

- (WAC) U.S. Women's Army Corps, 1944 - 1945
- Intelligence Security Officer

Esther Leach, a former school teacher, joined the WACs because, she said, "It was the thing to do." She remembered taking a gas mask with her to The Hill, where she served in the Security and Intelligence Office checking up on civilian employees. "I couldn't pronounce the Spanish names," she recalled.

She enjoyed a lot of activities: softball games, dances, movies (where one sat on benches), and hamburgers at the PX after dates.

Best Christmas Wishes and Happiness throughout the Year

Esther was a good dancer; often she and her dance partner were the center of attention.

Sunday brunch at Fuller Lodge, served 9 am to 2 pm, cost a dollar. She said she was glad to have been there at that time. "We saved a bunch of lives. It was what we were supposed to do." ✦

27

Edulia (Bustos) Bridge

- ✦ Worked January, 1943–November, 1946
- ✦ Lab technician and supervisor
- ✦ Made detonators for the bomb

Edulia Bustos came to Los Alamos from Seattle, Washington, where she had worked at the Boeing Company making military aircraft. She hadn't expected to be working in the mess hall; however, she said; she did just that—serving soldiers and WACs until her security clearance came through. Then she really went to work on the war effort.

She was first a lab technician; later she was promoted to supervisor. She says she soldered wires that were only one-one-thousandth of an inch in diameter. At the time, she was completely in the dark as to what she was working on. "We didn't ask questions. We just did what we were told."

Bridge had grown up in Santa Fe, so going home from Los Alamos during the week would have been easy; however she was only allowed to go home on weekends.

We couldn't talk about what we did," she said. "It was only after Hiroshima that we knew we had been working on the atom bomb." ✦

(Photo Courtesy of Los Alamos Historical Society Archives)

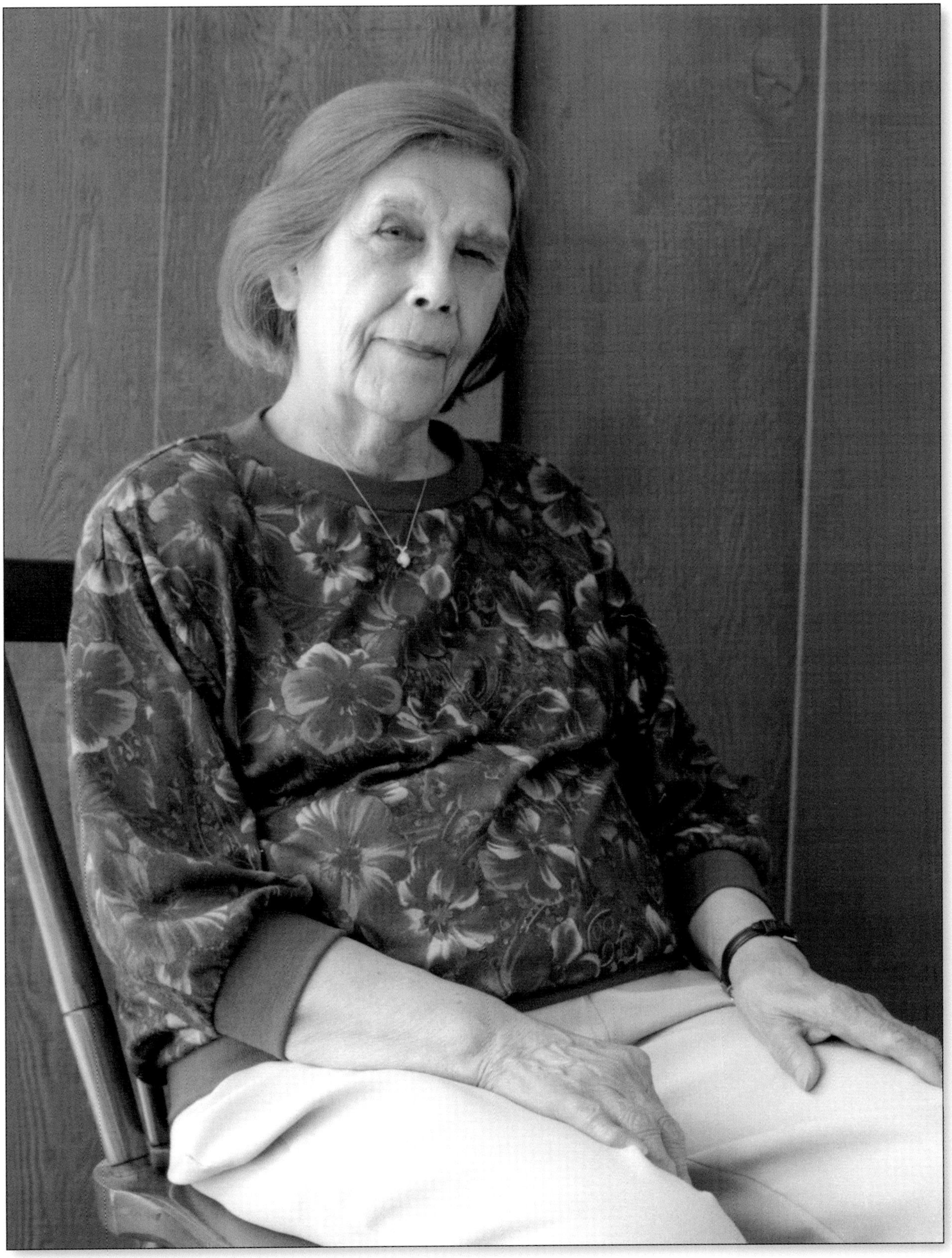

James "Jim" Andrew Bridge, civilian

- Worked May, 1943–1986
- Mechanical engineer
- Worked on measurements for the bomb

Jim Bridge came to work at the Lab because his older brother, a physicist, told him, "If you come to work at the Lab, one plane over Germany will end the war."

"That was enough to convince me," Bridge emphasized.

It happened one night at a Pojaque roadhouse, Jim recalls. A man who was a janitor at the Lab had too much to drink. He was spouting off, announcing his importance by what he thought he knew.

Holding up a resistor, he proclaimed to all of the occupants of the bar, "If you knew what this was, you wouldn't be within one hundred feet of it."

It was just bad luck for the janitor that night; a Lab security officer was in the audience. When the janitor returned to work after the weekend, he no longer had a job. Bridge concluded, "Security breaches were not to be tolerated by anyone, anytime." ✦

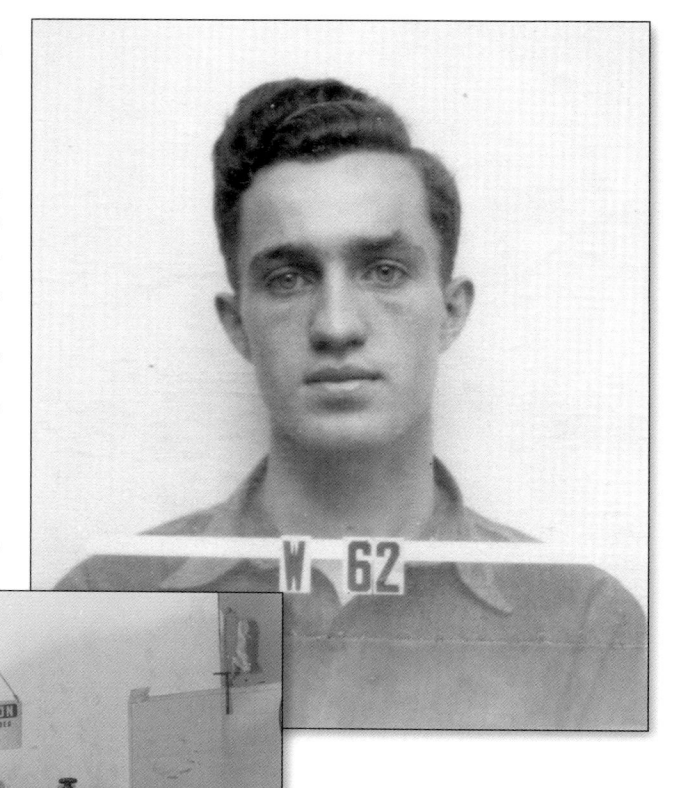

Robert Clark, left, with Jim Bridge *(Courtesy of Los Alamos National Lab Archives)*

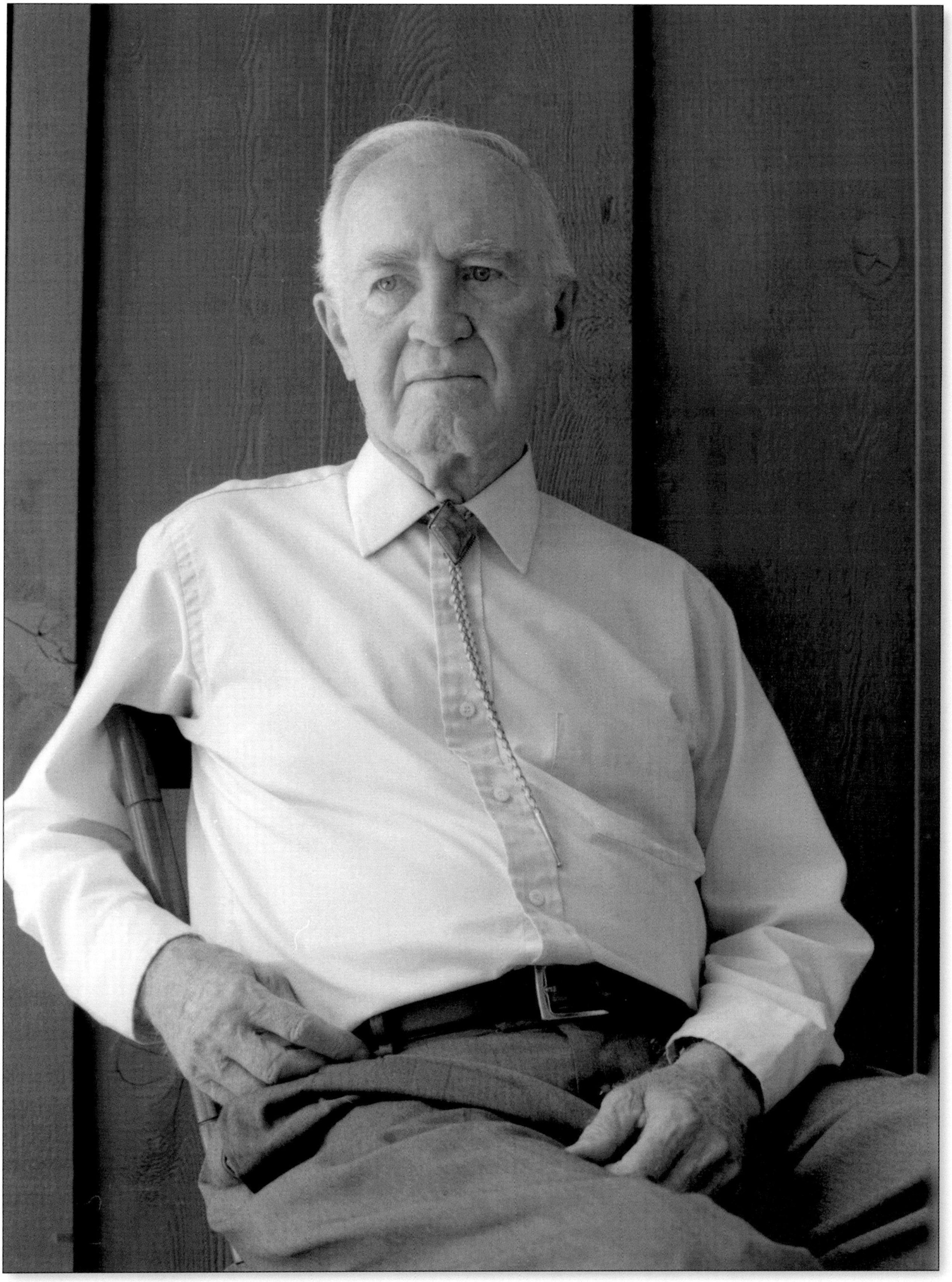

Berlyn Brixner, civilian

- ✦ Worked July, 1943–1978
- ✦ Photographer with U.S. Army Engineers

Coffee Story: This is a story that Kathleen Brixner, Berlyn Brixner's daughter, remembers. At the time of this writing, Berlyn Brixner's memory of times past has faded.

I remember an anecdote told to me by Mother. It happened in 1945, right after World War II but before many scientists had left The Hill to return to private life following the conclusion of The Manhattan Project.

The story was that Dad (Berlyn Brixner), Mom (Betty Brixner), Dick Feynman, Julian Mack and assorted others took a trip to Monument Valley, Arizona. In those days it was a desolate and remote place, to put it mildly—dirt roads, sometimes washed out, no people seen for endless miles in every direction, but, of course, fabulous red rock landscape, the reason for the trip. They traveled in two cars for safety because it was a very bad place to have a break down—absolutely no garage or services available.

Along the way they stopped to rest, build a campfire, and cook a pot of coffee. Soon, up on the tops of the surrounding hills, Navajos on horseback appeared herding sheep. Curious as to what these people were doing, the Navajos rode down from the ridge and happily joined the koffee klatch. Now this was *cowboy coffee*: a big pot filled with water, brought to a boil, removed from the fire, then coffee dumped in to brew. After the grounds obligingly settled to the bottom in a few minutes, *ta da*...the coffee was ready to drink!

With the extra people, another pot was put on, boiled, removed, and coffee added. But one of the Navajo guests picked up the one-pound can (remember those?) and, with a big smile, dumped the remaining coffee in, making the brew strong enough to please his taste!

In an age of wartime commodity shortages, this seemed extravagant; but hospitality demanded no complaint be made. Everyone, surprisingly, found it quite a delicious cup! When the last drop was drunk, the guests mounted their horses and departed over the ridge, not to be seen again for the rest of the adventure.

(No one said if anyone ever made "Navajo coffee" again.) ✦

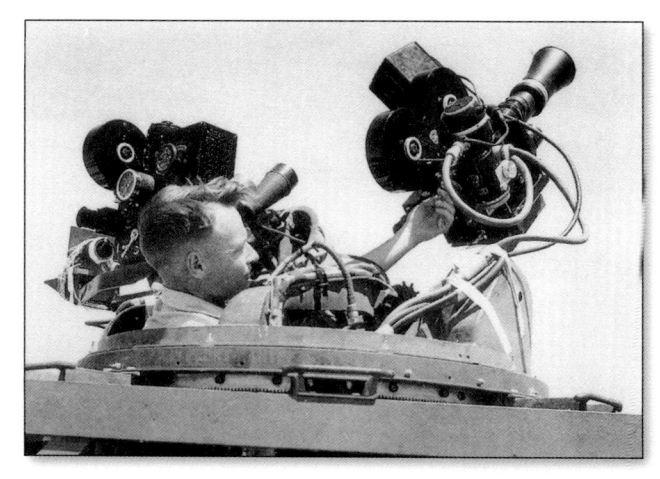

Berlyn Brixner with the high-speed camera he designed and built—used for photographing explosion experiments.

Ben Benjamin, (left), and Berlyn Brixner
(Courtesy of Los Alamos National Lab Archives)

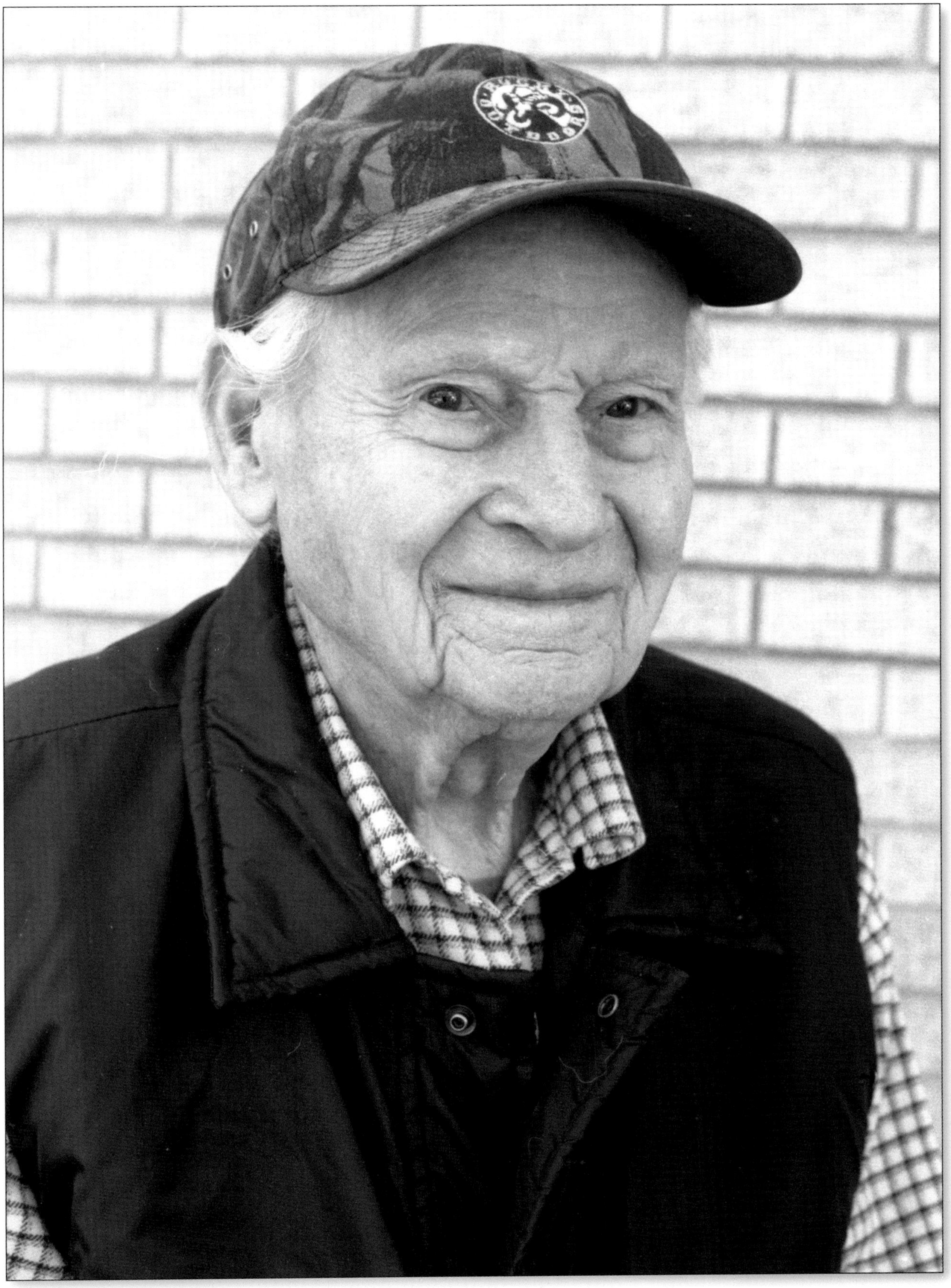

Margaret "Beebe" Caldes

✦ Worked 1943–1946
✦ Secretary

Beebe Caldes worked first as a stock clerk, then as secretary for Julian Mack in the photography department. "I found the work interesting, and I understood it since my father was a professional photographer."

Beebe Caldes recalls an amusing incident: her boss was trying to get a phone call connected. He yelled, "Beebe, diddle the operator." Caldes said no one else knew what he was talking about or why. He had lost the connection and wanted her to get in touch with the operator.

She also remembers being chased around the office by the G.I.'s one day. She escaped however.

The Caldeses were the first, other than the Military Police, to have horses on The Hill. They even built their own corral and shed, and enjoyed exploring the surrounding mountains on horseback.

It was not often that occupants of Los Alamos could get a weekend away. One weekend, she and her husband did manage that. But they were followed by a security man who stationed himself just outside their hotel room. So much for a weekend alone.

"Security was tight. We did what we were told and didn't ask questions. We knew it was important for the war." ✦

Julian Mack *(Courtesy of Los Alamos Historical Society Archives)*

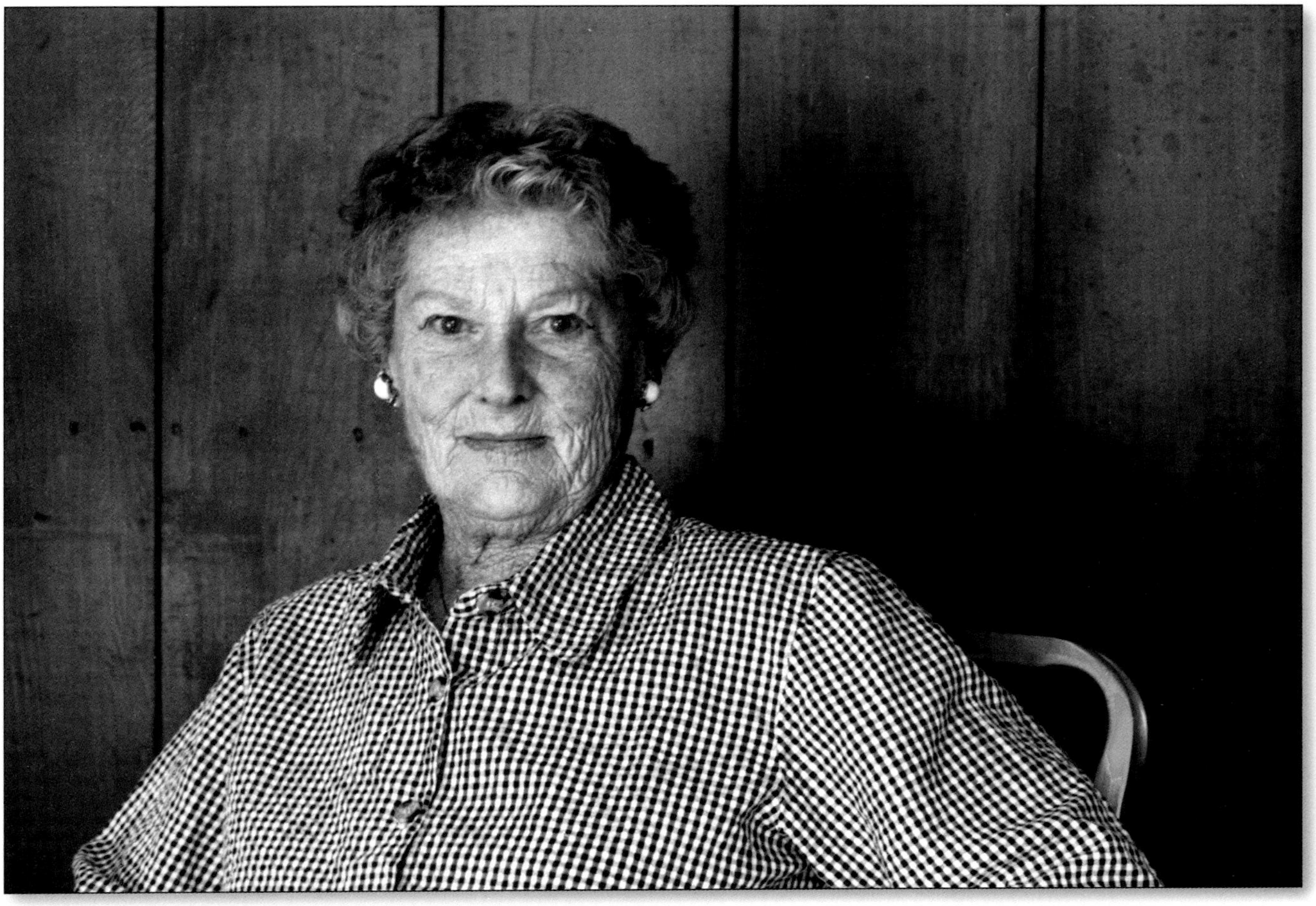

William "Bill" Caldes, civilian

- ✦ Physicist, worked April, 1943–1949
- ✦ Electronic instrumentation for the bomb
- ✦ Transferred to Sandia Lab 1949, retired 1983

The nineteenth person on The Hill, Bill Caldes transferred from the Laboratory of Scientific Research and Development at Princeton University to Los Alamos. Caldes remembers what a task it was to get a letter delivered to someone outside. He had to send the letter to Princeton so that it could be postmarked and mailed from there. When he received mail, it was sent to Princeton and forwarded to him at Los Alamos. Security was tight; no one, other than people on The Hill and his former supervisors at Princeton, knew he was not at Princeton.

When Caldes became engaged to his girlfriend of five years, security personnel said he would have to be married on The Hill; he would not be allowed to leave to be married in Princeton. Caldes went to Oppenheimer for a reprieve. Since the Lab was not even set up yet, Oppie told him he could get married at Princeton. Caldes left immediately for twelve days.

When the couple returned, without even a honeymoon, there was no housing for them, so they spent a week at Del Monte Ranch (now, Four Seasons Resort Rancho Encantado Santa Fe) and then went to Bandelier to live.

"If it were not for Oppie, we wouldn't have gotten married," asserted Caldes, who has been married to Beebe since June, 1943.

Caldes was with Enrico Fermi, the Italian scientist working on the project, for the test of the atomic bomb at Trinity Site. "My initial reaction was that this was the end of the world. The light was so brilliant you had to put your hands in front of your eyes, but your eyes were still burning." ✦

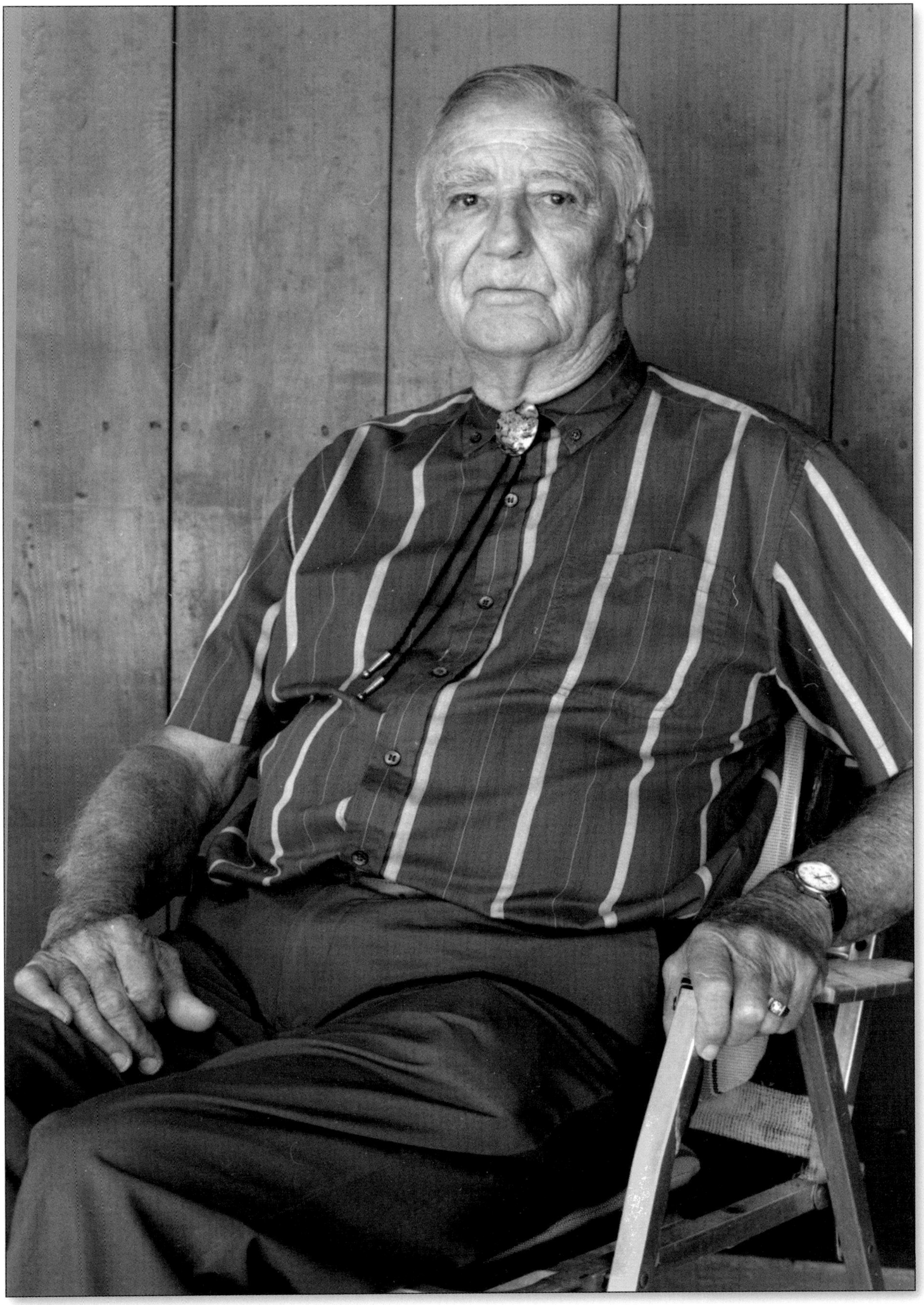

Bengt Carlson, civilian

- ✦ Worked June 4, 1945–1976
- ✦ Specialties in mathematical physics, math, and computers
- ✦ Solved equations in theoretical decisions as they occurred

Bengt Carlson, his wife Julia, and eight-month-old son came to the Lab from Montreal, Quebec, in a '37 Willys Overland coupe, which stalled on its first trip up The Hill. He had bought the car when he was at U.C. Berkeley in 1943 for the huge sum of $90 and named it "Bambi."

The family set up housekeeping in a duplex where their next-door neighbor was Roger Wescott who told the Carlsons, "I don't see how you made it across country in that car!"

One day when Carlson returned from work, he was horrified to find the engine of his coupe spread out in his front yard in what seemed like a million pieces. Wescott had disassembled it and was working it over. Eventually Bambi received a completely rebuilt engine that included new valves.

Wescott said he had always been interested in cars and liked to "fiddle with them." After Wescott performed the life-saving surgery on Bambi, she performed much better. ✦

(Courtesy of Los Alamos National Lab Archives)

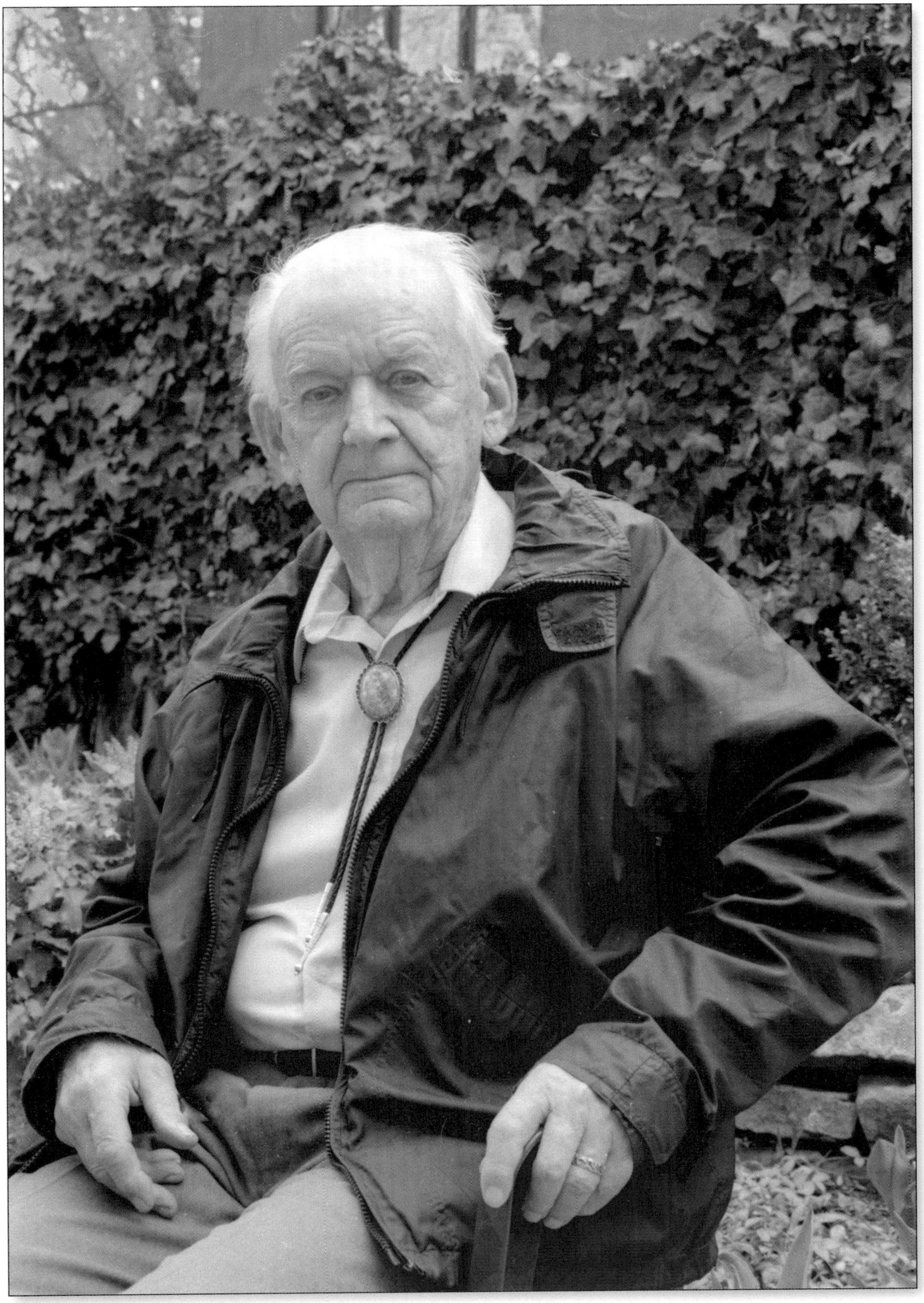

Beatrice (Dasheno) Chavarria

- Santa Clara Pueblo, Christmas holiday, 1944
- Worked as housekeeper in the dorms

Bea Dasheno was one of several young school girls from St. Catherine's Indian School in Santa Fe who worked on The Hill during the war.

"When I found out about the atom bomb after Hiroshima, I really felt sorry for the poor people who died or were hurt during the bombing. I was disappointed to learn that making a bomb was what was being done at Los Alamos."

After the war, Chavarria worked for several Los Alamos families who had moved to Pajarito Village near Santa Clara Pueblo. Among those families was the Schreiber family. Marge Schreiber has kept in touch with Chavarria over the years. ✦

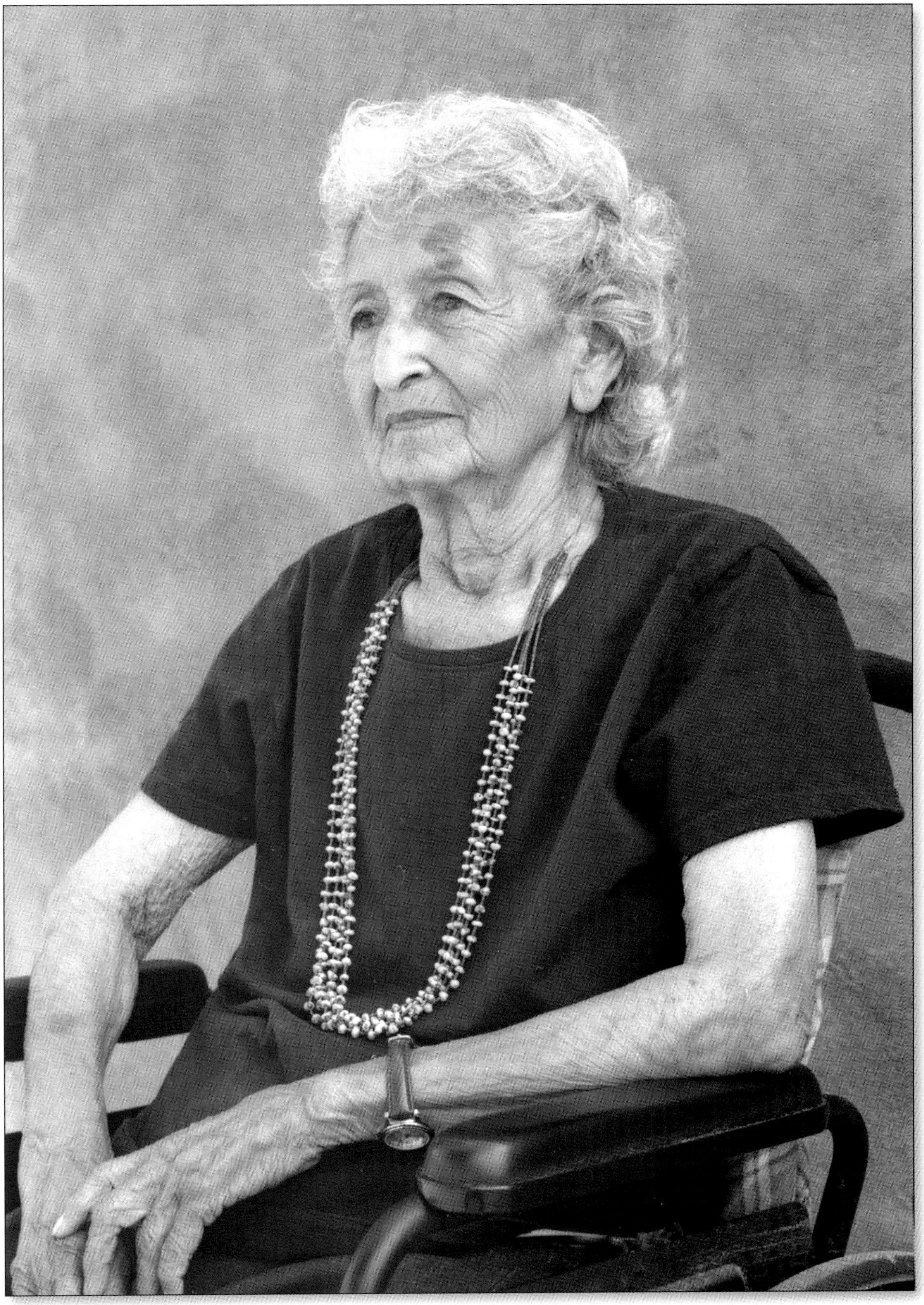

Consuelo "Connie" (Meyer) Chouinard

- ✦ Worked summers, 1945 and 1946
- ✦ Christmas holiday, 1944
- ✦ Mail and copying records

Connie Meyer came to The Hill from Las Vegas, New Mexico, with Mary Lou Maloney (now Michnovicz). She took a typing and clerical test and was hired during her college summer vacation.

Forbidden to look at what she was copying, Meyer said MPs emptied the waste baskets immediately after she copied records so as not to breach security.

But she said, "I am a fast reader and I did read them." Through reading a classified file, Connie remembers how horrified she was when she found out that a friend of a relative in Las Vegas had a husband who was in charge of a communist cell. She couldn't tell anyone that it existed because she was not supposed to have read the classified file.

The MPs made certain she took nothing out of the workroom with her. "You were searched and you couldn't even take a purse. You only had a certain amount of time to go to the bathroom and to lunch." ✦

Connie Meyer (left), **with Mary Lou Maloney** (right)

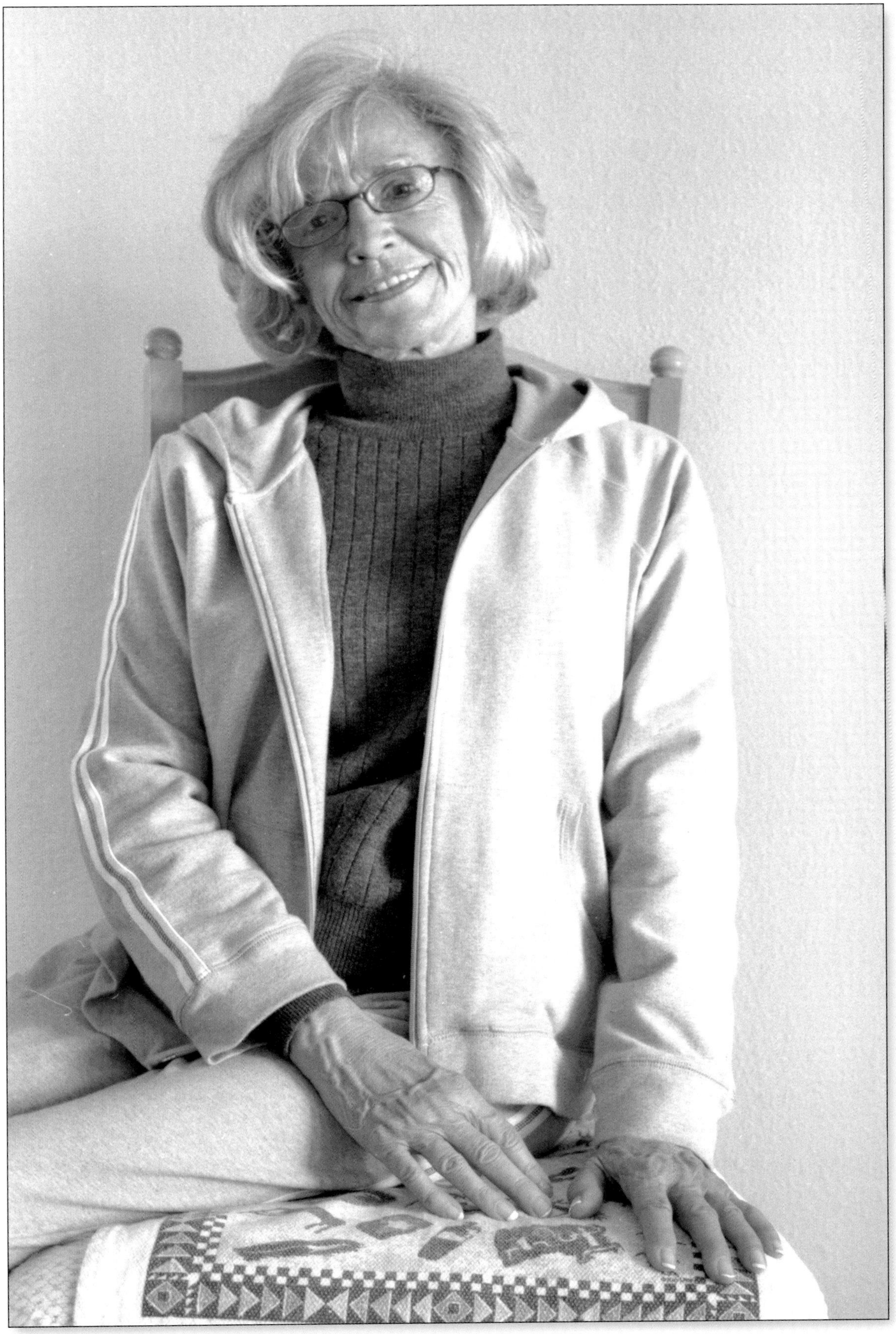

Helen "Satch" (Dunham) Cowan

✦ Physical chemist, worked 1945–1980
✦ Assayed plutonium

New Mexico was no surprise to Helen Dunham when she arrived on The Hill in 1945. In 1932 she and her parents were touring in New Mexico. Their visits included Springer, Taos and Santa Fe. "I knew what New Mexico was like," she declared. "I had climbed the mountains in this state."

Dunham first worked at the Metallurgical Lab at the University of Chicago and was later sent to Los Alamos. Many people whom she knew at the Chicago lab disappeared, and she knew they had transferred to other sites such as Oak Ridge, Tennessee, and Hanford, Washington, as well as Los Alamos. "I knew they were working on the bomb," she confided.

"When I arrived in Santa Fe, I boarded an army bus to take me up to The Hill. I noticed that the bus followed a new, shiny, copper electrical wire," she went on. "There were no guard rails along the unpaved road, and I could look down into the canyon—a bit intimidating."

Supposedly, Dunham was to have a private room. However, the dorm had not yet been constructed so she had a roommate. It was quite an unwelcome shock that first night to learn that the roommate had just been notified that her husband had been killed in the war.

(Photo by John "Mike Michnovicz)

At the Lab, Helen met many of her old friends from the University of Chicago. And, ironically, although steak in Chicago was pretty scarce, it was plentiful at Los Alamos, a welcome change—if you had the food stamps to buy the meat.

She remembers how many people disappeared in July from the Lab to Trinity Site at Alamogordo. The only women who went to observe the test had husbands who were scientists. That left Dunham out; she had to wait at Los Alamos.

She waited for quite a while and nothing was happening. About the time she was ready to head for home, as it was quite early in the morning, she suddenly saw a brilliant light in the sky and then the mushroom cloud. "I was so excited to learn that it actually worked," she related.

"I wouldn't trade my experiences here for anything," she emphasized. "Being at Los Alamos has enriched my life. I understand more things because of these experiences."

Cowan is an avid hiker and a swimmer. "I have taught hundreds of kids to swim," she concluded. ✦

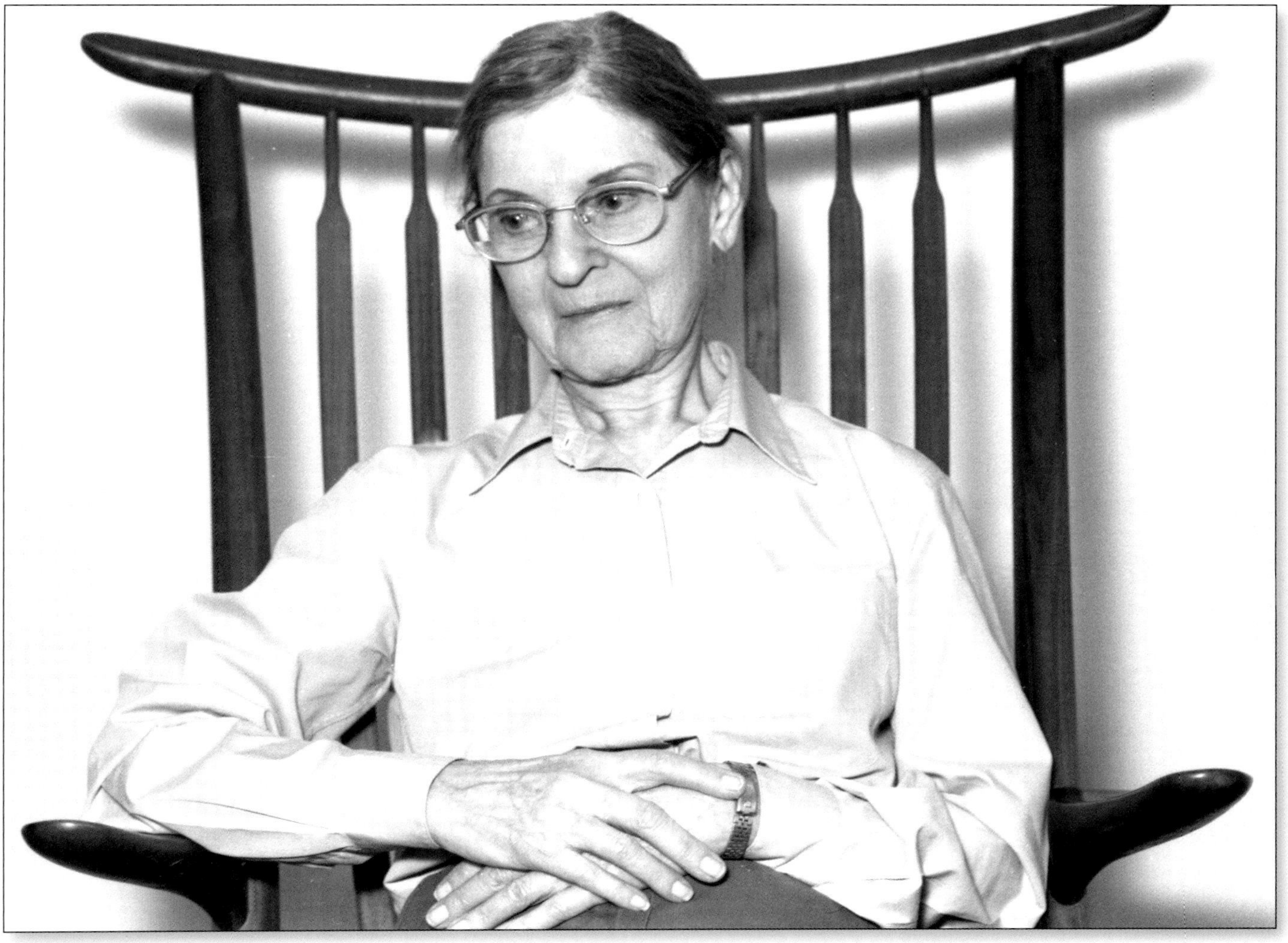

Marian (Long) Cox

✦ (WAC) U.S. Women's Army Corps, early 1943–November, 1945
✦ Procurement

Not all of the experiences on The Hill were pleasant. Marian Cox remembered an incident when she, a date, Reed Cameron, and another couple went to Santa Fe for a day in the "Big City."

A car driven by WAC Eleanor Cuthbertson was to pick up Harry Allen's wife (Allen was procurement officer) at the Albuquerque airport and take her to Los Alamos. "The four of us got a ride from Santa Fe in that car since it had to come through Santa Fe anyway in those days," Cox recalled. "Four of us were wedged into the backseat. I was sitting on my date's lap since there was not much room. We headed up the road and all seemed well at first."

But suddenly the car veered off the road and actually crashed into a large boulder. That was fortunate since it kept the car from careening down the steep mountainside, Cox reported.

"Reed shoved me away from the window, so I was not hurt. The other girl in the back was not so fortunate; she got her foot caught under the back of the front seat and received serious pelvic injuries." It was really scary," Cox went on. "I think Eleanor fell asleep at the wheel." No one else seemed to be seriously hurt.

"The other WAC who was with me in the back received a medical discharge and left Los Alamos," Cox concluded. ✦

(Photo by John "Mike" Michnovicz)

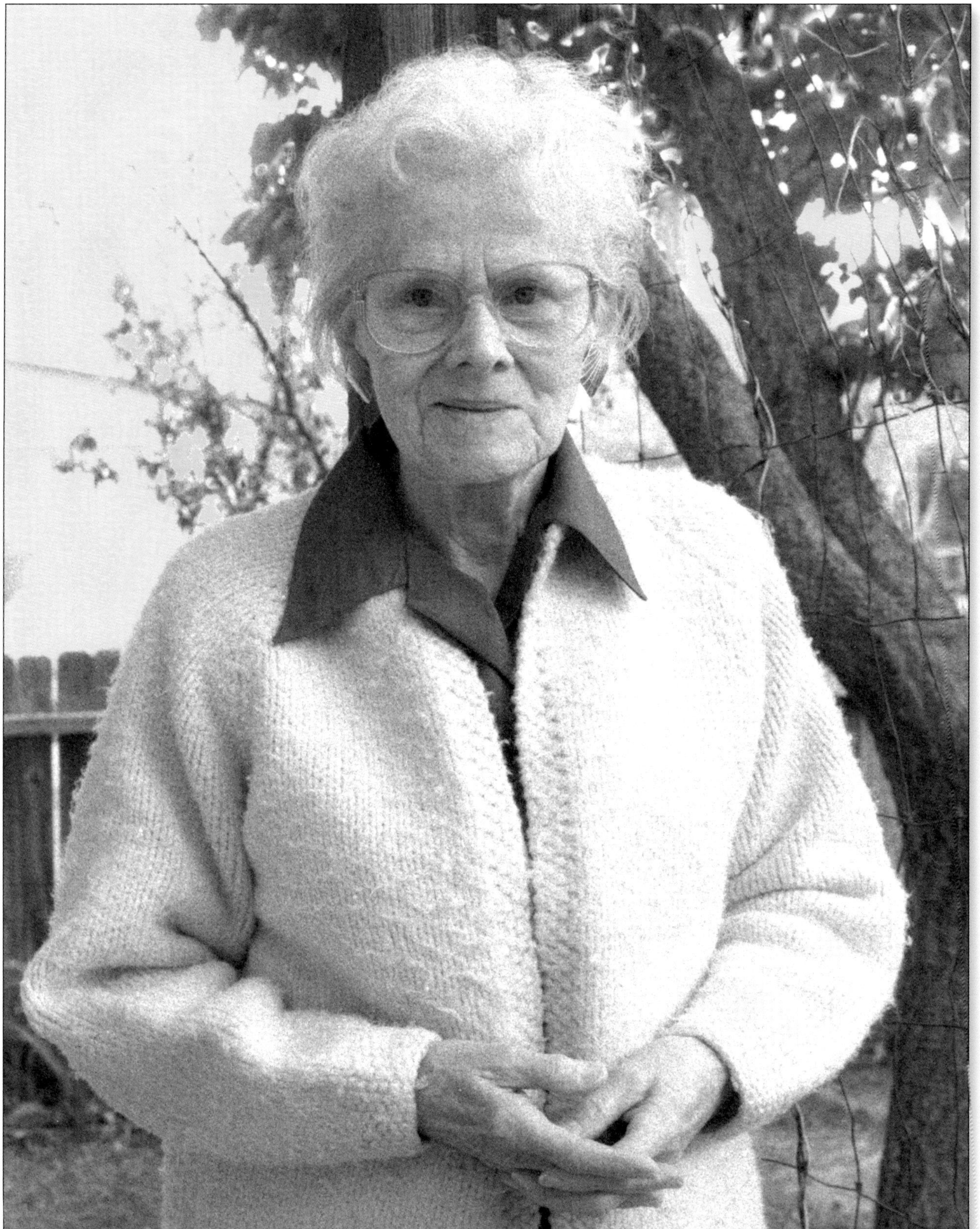

Jean (Waiter) Dabney

- (WAC) U.S. Women's Army Corps, First Sergeant, July, 1943–August, 1945
- Electronics technician
- Built electronics equipment to be used in testing the bomb

Jean Waiter and her husband-to-be, Winston "Dab" Dabney, had a difficult time keeping even their first date. The fates seemed to be against them.

A WAC friend of Jean's who worked in Dabney's section, became the go-between. Dab was intrigued by Jean, the pretty little WAC, and wanted to meet her. She wasn't dating anyone at that time and decided to take a look at him.

They made a date to meet at the coffee shop. However, Jean had to be at the testing site that evening. She told Dab that if the experiment did not go well, she might have to stay late. It didn't, and stay late she did. She didn't leave the testing site until 3 am, missing her date—date number one a miss-fire.

Not to be discouraged, they made another date to meet at the coffee shop. But again, it was not to be. Dab had to drive his captain to Santa Fe, so the meeting fell through again—date number two another miss-fire.

The third date really happened. Jean and Dab met at the coffee shop and had the date—finally. "It was meant to be," Jean emphasized.

They had a real Los Alamos and New Mexico courtship and wedding. The couple was married at the La Fonda Hotel in Santa Fe on August 18, 1945. Winston managed two three-day passes and they had a honeymoon in Red River, New Mexico. It's fortunate that they persevered. Jean and Dab now have been married more than sixty years (in 2006).

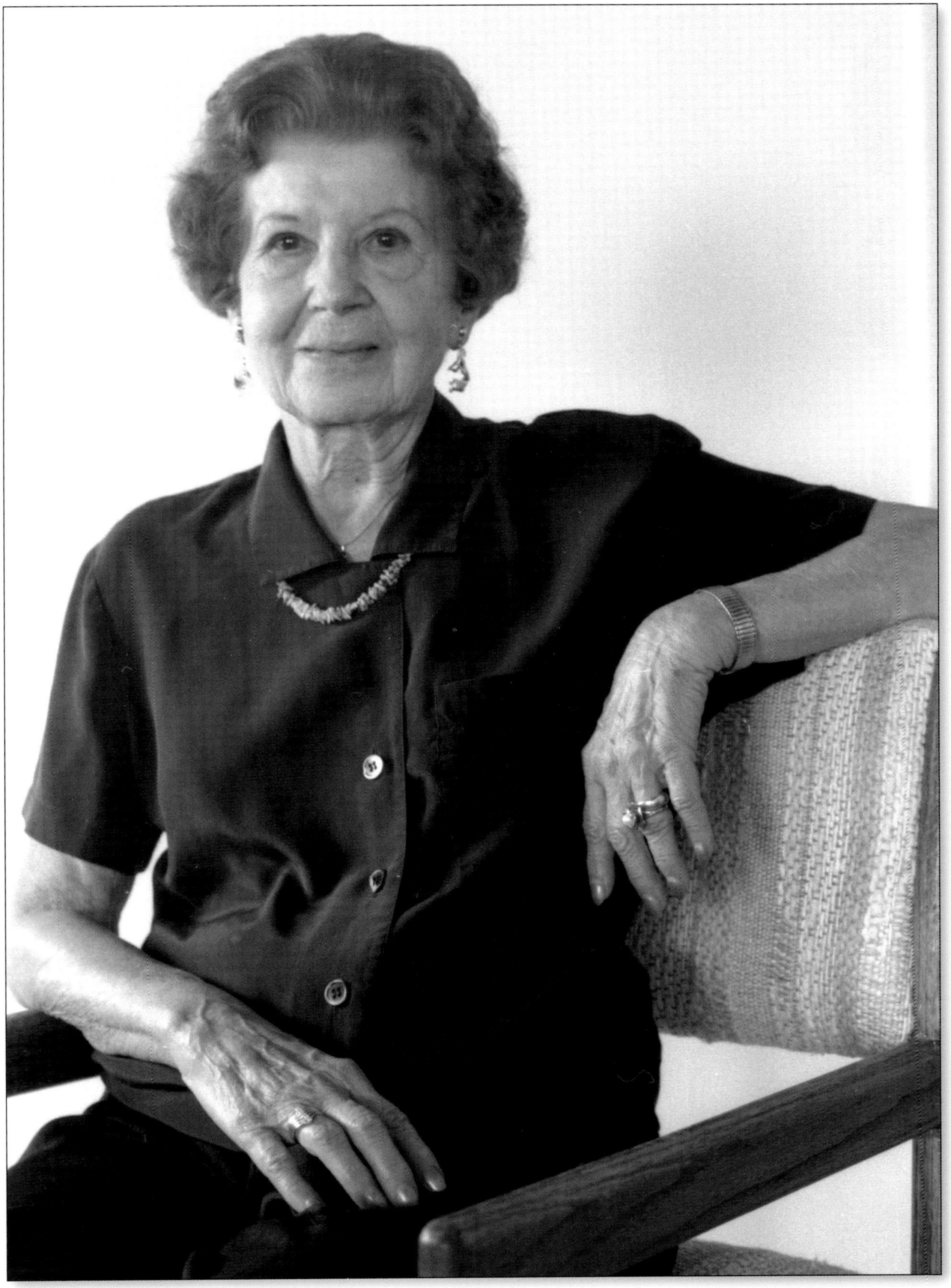

Neil Davis, U.S. Army, Tech Sergeant

- ✦ (SED) Special Engineer Detachment, January, 1945–February, 1946
- ✦ Civilian employee February, 1946–May, 1993
- ✦ Electrical engineer—Built electronics equipment

Neil Davis came to Los Alamos when he was twenty-one years old, fresh out of the University of Texas (Austin), and was assigned to an electronics group. The group built electronics equipment starting with just pieces since no suitable commercial equipment was available. "You could buy only vacuum tubes," Davis noted. Davis said that many of the designers in his group were from Britain.

He fondly remembers the music and dances at the NCO (non-commissioned officers) Club. "There were no private vehicles in camp and consequently not much dating." he pointed out. "People just showed up, although there were some attachments."

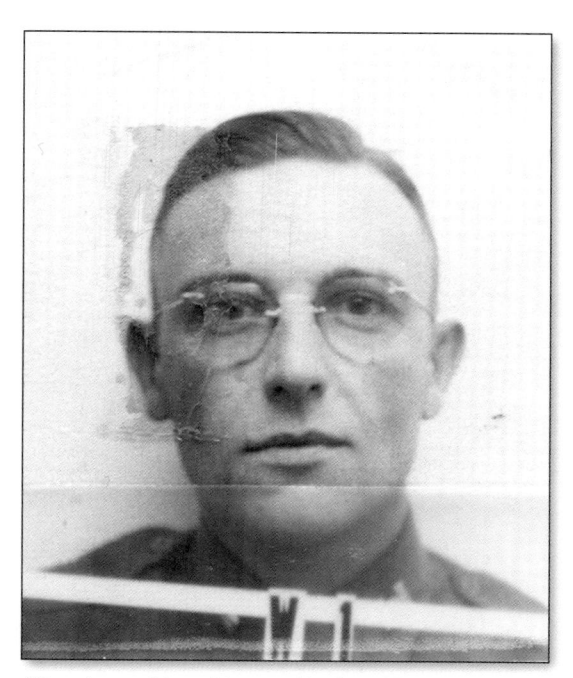

(Courtesy of Los Alamos National Lab Archives)

(Courtesy of Los Alamos National Lab Archives)

About his work on the bomb, Davis was adamant. "It would stop the war if it worked, and I had no regrets at the time and certainly none afterwards. It was worth it, even with the innocent civilian casualties in Japan. In the long run, the atomic bomb saved a lot of lives."

In 1984 Davis went to Japan. At Hiroshima he visited the Peace Park where few Westerners ever went. "We were quite conspicuous, and people somehow knew we were from Los Alamos. However, we were treated very well." ✦

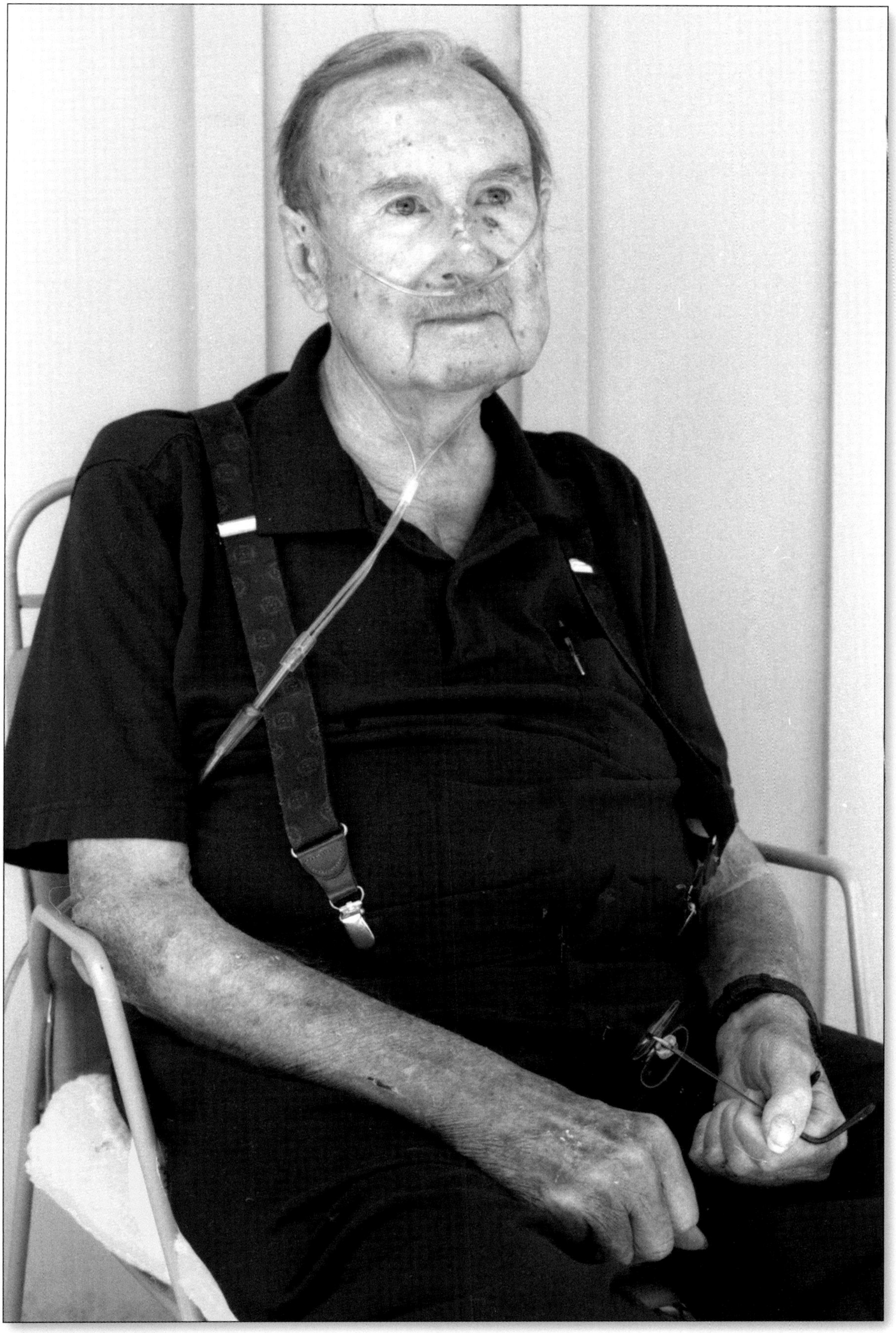

Margaret Dike

- Worked Spring, 1944–December, 1945
- Reports editor for Electronics Section
- Secretary-draftsman, Chemistry Section
- Engineering draftsman

Margaret Dike remembers the living conditions she found herself in, on The Hill in 1944. "We lived in a quadraplex which was heated by a coal furnace. There was plenty of coal dust and smoke, but fortunately the furnace was stoked and maintained by others."

She says the kitchen had a two-burner hot plate—no stove. "You could use a portable oven though. We got a roaster oven and often cooked for the G.I.s, who were glad to have something other than mess hall food."

In June, 1945, Margaret and her husband, Sheldon Dike, notified officials that they were going to Corkin's Lodge, a resort near Chama, New Mexico, for a vacation. "We had a couple of nice days alone together and then the vacation ended abruptly. A car arrived to take Sheldon back—with no warning. There were no telephones at Corkin's Lodge.

Sheldon was then sent overseas to Tinian's Island with the Bomb Group. His work was with the drop-mechanism modifications of the B-29 bombers.

About the atomic bombing of Hiroshima, Dike says she has mixed feelings. It was a way to end the war, but it was tragic to devastate an entire city; however, we would have lost thousands of troops if an invasion had been necessary.

(Courtesy of Los Alamos National Lab Archives)

Maybe we saved more by ending it quickly, but who knows?"

Dike moved to Albuquerque, where she has received numerous awards for her many civic activities. Included is the New Mexico Lifetime Achievement Award that she received in 2002. That was the first time the award had been given to a woman.

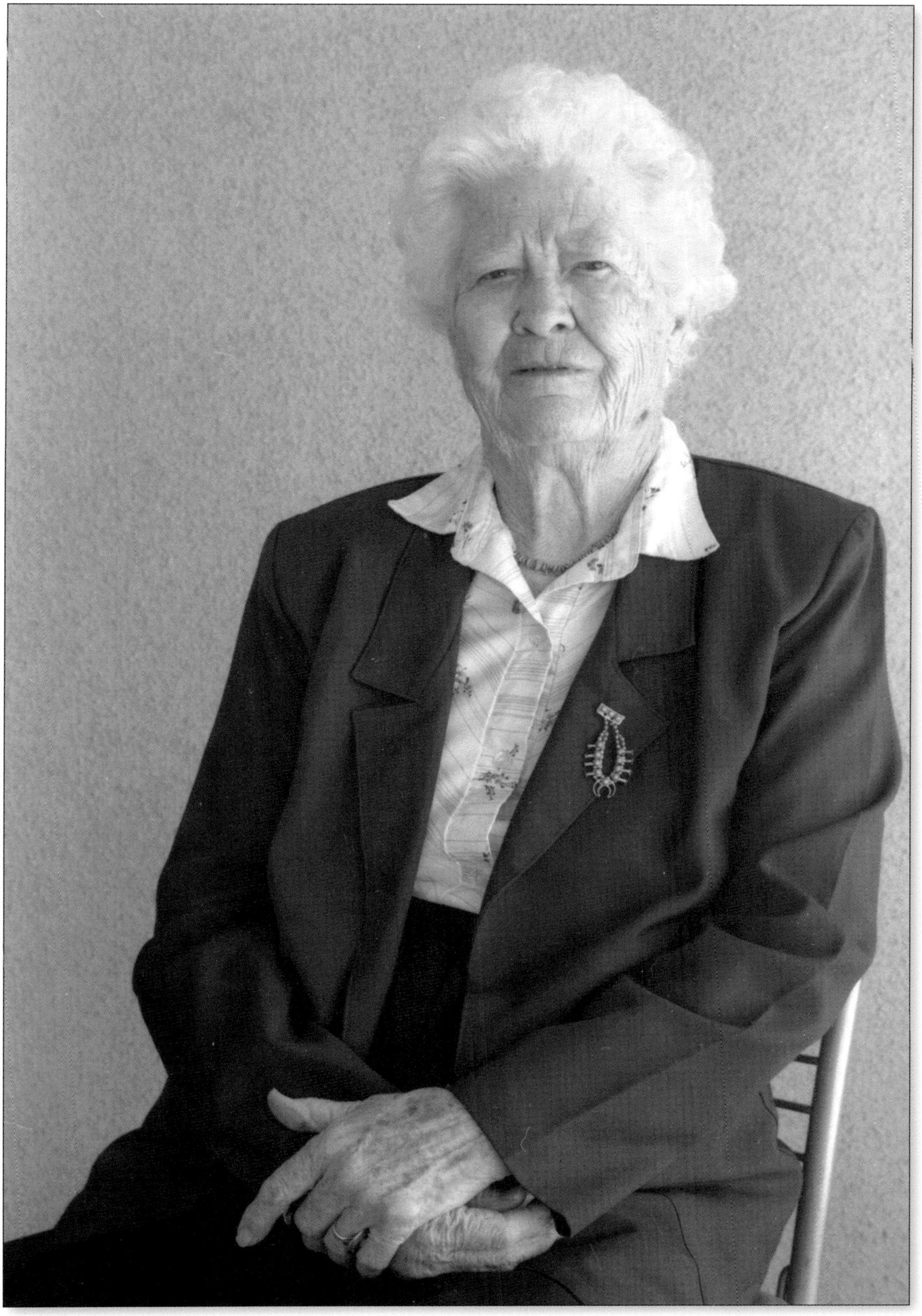

Benjamin "Ben" Diven, civilian

+ Physicist, worked March, 1943–1977
+ Worked at several jobs including making instrumentation for nuclear physics measurements for others to use

Ben Diven was one of the first people on The Hill, having been recruited by Oppenheimer at University of California at Berkeley in the fall of 1942. In early March of '43, he traveled to Los Alamos as part of the advance party.

"There was just this terrible big cloud of dust on The Hill at that time," Diven noted, "and I was just a handyman because nothing was completed." Diven said he took care of the truckloads of lab equipment because there were no buildings ready for installation of the equipment.

The person who was supposed to take care of purchasing and deliveries had not arrived, so Diven assumed the responsibility of finding a place to warehouse the flood of deliveries.

Only one building was completed and empty, and it was reserved for a future project. In the interim this building became a temporary warehouse for deliveries from all over the United States.

Gradually, important scientists and technicians began arriving and setting up their particular labs as the buildings were completed.

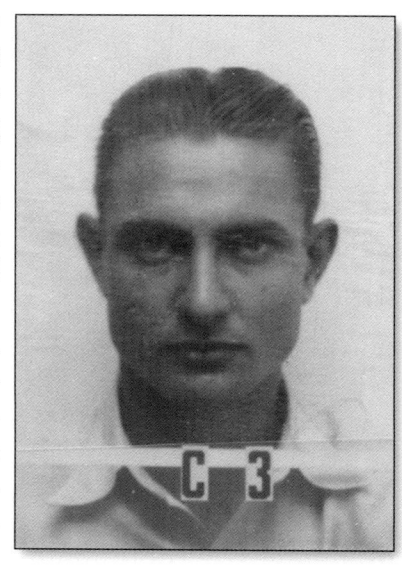

(Courtesy of Los Alamos National Lab Archives)

However, only one truck was available to make deliveries from the warehouse—a large dump truck.

One day, a group of scientists and technicians came to the warehouse to pick up parts for the cyclotron they were to assemble. They carefully loaded the parts into the truck. Then they climbed inside the cab and prepared to leave with their supplies. Unfortunately, not one of them had ever driven a dump truck before. One of the men pushed a wrong button and, bingo, the truck did its thing: it efficiently dumped all of the equipment on the ground.

Diven said he didn't stay around to see what they were going to do about it." I was too busy to worry about that," he said. "It was their job to get it loaded up again. Other people needed that truck too."

Obviously, they did finally get the cyclotron assembled and working—or the Manhattan Project would not have been successful. ✦

(Courtesy of Los Alamos National Lab Archives)

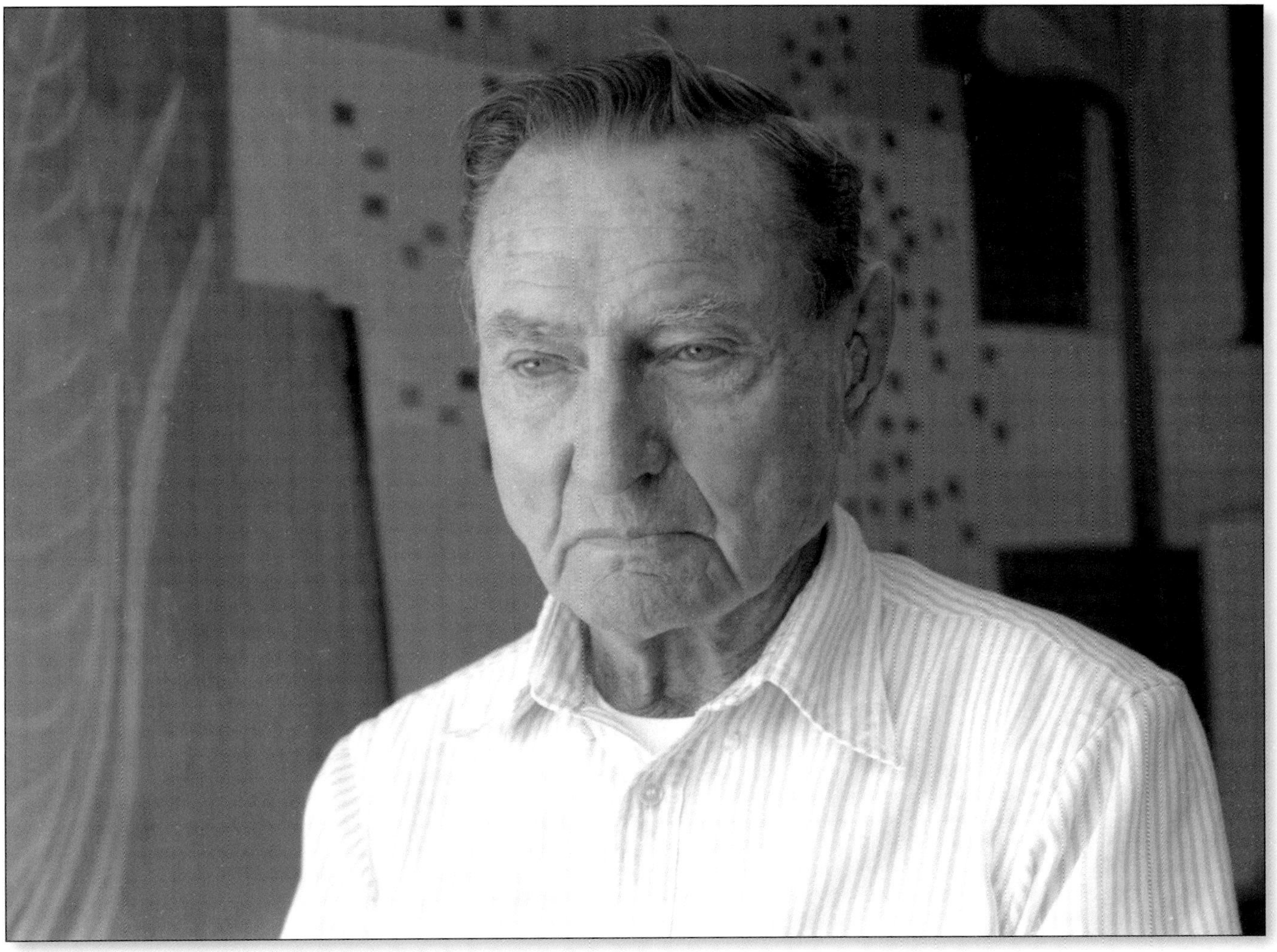

Rebecca "Beckie" (Bradford) Diven

✦ Worked 1944–1951
✦ Various jobs in chemistry

Beckie Bradford came to The Hill from a position at the University of California at Berkeley. Her first job was weighing minute amounts of plutonium. When the supply of plutonium became more plentiful, she was trained to radio-assay plutonium.

She recalls her "priority" dormitory room which, was so-classified because it had a bath between two bedrooms while other (non-priority) dorms had one bath per floor. The room was a scant nine by twelve feet. The closet had no door. The furnishings consisted of a cot, and a desk and chair—no lamps, no curtains, no bedspread.

The dormitory had ten rooms upstairs and ten down. Rent was $15 a month including maid service; linens were changed weekly. Dorm residents were women of different ages and different careers. There were secretaries, mathematicians, chemists, electronics specialists, and a hematologist.

Bradford set to work to make her room her own nest. She sent word to Dorothy McKibbin in Santa Fe to get material and spools of thread to make curtains and a bedspread. McKibbin was in charge of the clearance office which issued the passes needed to go up to The Hill; she was also problem solver and first friend to everyone at Los Alamos.

Diven said, "Dorothy was wonderful. She would get whatever you needed and send it up. You could walk in on Dorothy at her office at 109 E. Palace Ave., and even if she were busy, she would stop what she was doing and pay complete attention to you. You felt as if you were the most important person in the world to Dorothy. She was a really warm person."

And now for fun: Diven said that when the MPs were not patrolling the premises on horseback, you could ride one of the horses—if you could catch it. I never did real well at that," she reminisced, "because I never really know how to ride. I handled the reins like a steering wheel and it didn't work very well," she concluded. ✦

(Courtesy of Los Alamos National Lab Archives)

(Courtesy of Los Alamos Historical Society Archives)

Diven is 5th from left *(Courtesy of Los Alamos Historical Society Archives)*

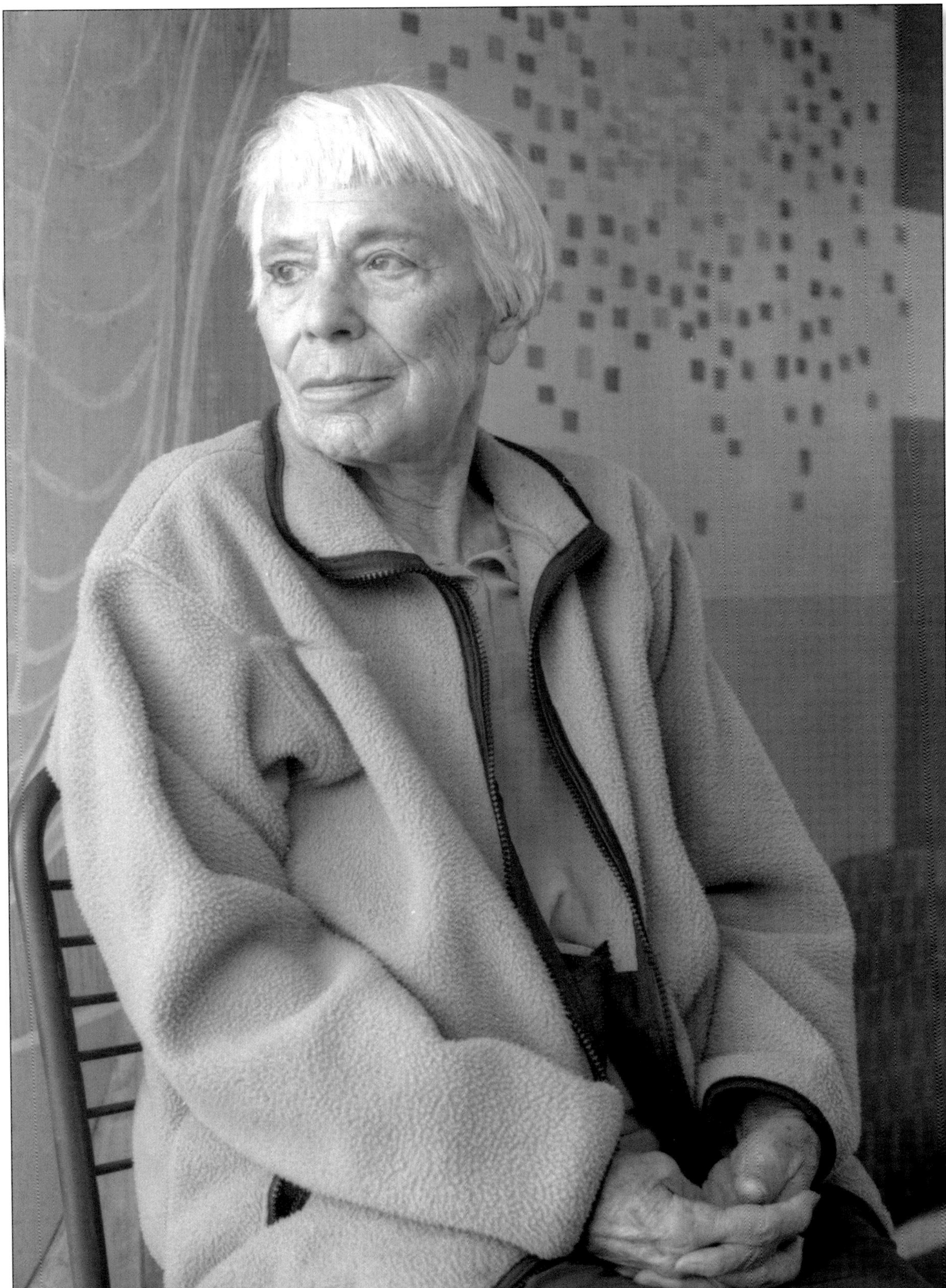

Charlotte (Hagman) Duran

- Lived on The Hill March, 1944–August, 1945
- Sixth grade elementary student

Charlotte Hagman did not like all the moving around she had to do with her family—and she certainly didn't like moving to The Hill. In fact she cried about this move. The family moved into a two-bedroom, one-bath wooden duplex, she said. Her mother worked at the laundry. Her dad was a plumber in the tech area; he had to wear booties over his shoes so that if there were any contamination, he would not track it out.

"Right after we moved in March, my sister Thelma and I were sent to the grocery store—but we couldn't find it so returned home without the items." Charlotte was looking for a Safeway, but the only store was the commissary. She knew better the next time.

One day she went to the refrigerator to get some cold water. She poured herself a big glass and began to gulp it. "I thought I would die," she recalls. "It was not water but Everclear (pure alcohol). No alcohol was sold in Los Alamos except 3.2% beer, and I still am not sure where Dad got the Everclear."

She remembers her sixth-grade school days with teacher Jean Parks. Parks, who had Greek ancestry, was always coming up with plays about Greece for the class to perform. The students wrote and performed *Helen of Troy* in which Parks played Medusa. "We used cheesecloth for the costumes which we tie-dyed and helped make ourselves. We always had a lot of Greek gods and goddesses in our plays." Parks herself paid for the material and other items used in the plays, Duran noted. The teacher made a lasting impression on her student, and they kept in touch. ✦

Charlotte Duran (left) **with sister Thelma**

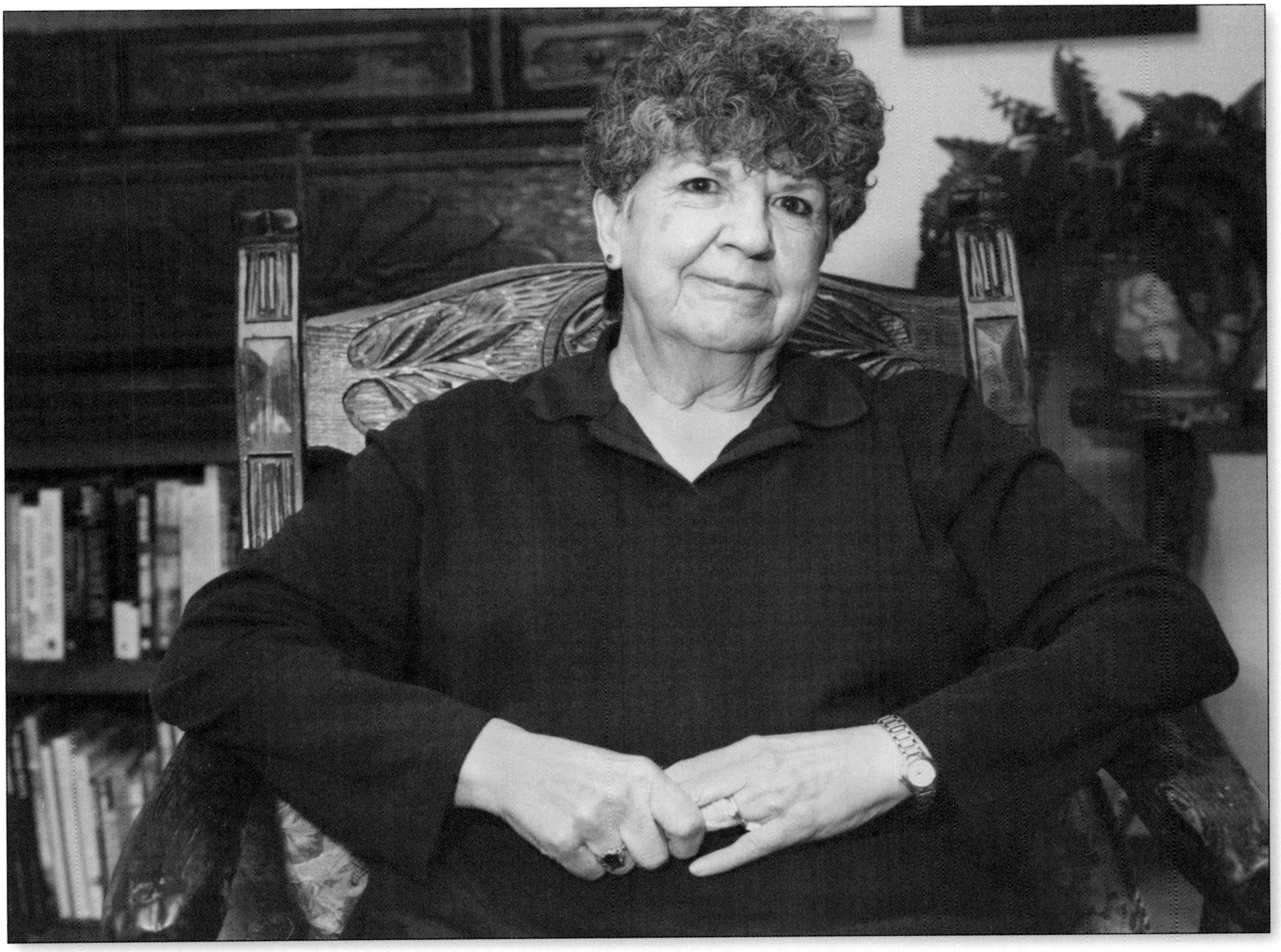

Hal Fishbine, U.S. Army

✦ (SED) Special Engineer Detachment, March 25, 1944–1946
✦ Civilian employee July, 1947–April, 1982
✦ Worked on x-ray machine research on imploding spheres

Transferred from the military base in San Francisco, Hal Fishbine arrived sleepy-eyed in New Mexico at 3 am, only to learn that his journey was not yet at an end.

"I was routed from San Francisco via train to Belen, New Mexico. From Belen I took a one-car diesel freight passenger train to Albuquerque. From Albuquerque, I took a bus that made stops on the way to Santa Fe. The train agent was a wartime employee who had little experience with passenger routing. Probably thought that Santa Fe was in a foreign country."

He could not rest until the bus deposited him at his destination on The Hill, where he was assigned to C Barracks.

Bonnie and Hal Fishbine
(Courtesy of Los Alamos Historical Society Archives)

(Courtesy of Los Alamos Historical Society Archives)

At Los Alamos, he found to his surprise, the makeshift ambience of The Hill: muddy streets, no sidewalks, thrown-together buildings. But most of all, he was surprised to learn that G.I. rules did not apply here—no one had to salute. That was a welcome change from the usual military base regulations.

Fishbine came with experience in repairing radios; however, that was not his only ability. He had studied music extensively, playing the violin and the bass viola. In fact, he had played with the Dick Jacob's Lucky Strike Band on the radio before the war.

Therefore when he heard discordant sounds coming from Theater Number Two, it was *not* music to his ears. He decided to investigate. An orchestra was rehearsing, but badly. Subsequently Fishbine was asked to organize a G.I. orchestra. He was able to recruit a sufficient number of talented G.I.s to form a thirteen-piece swing band. (Do you remember the jitterbug?)

The swing band practiced long and hard for their debut performance. The first dance was held in late November, near the Thanksgiving holiday. The newly-formed swing band was led by Fishbine, who also played the bass. An added musical attraction was the *Sad Sack Six* who jammed for the delighted and enthusiastic crowd in the middle of the evening.

Said Fishbine wryly, "Church services were held in the same hall the next day. I don't think they ever got the smell of beer out." [Not a holy Sunday morning aroma...]

The band continued performing after the war. At the 1945 Fiesta de Santa Fe, it was the only swing band. In 1946 they played for a New Year's Eve dance in the armory at Gallup, New Mexico. At the One-Hundredth Anniversary Celebration of J. Robert Oppenheimer's birth, in Los Alamos in April, 2004, Fishbine played the bass and, with a group of other musicians, provided the music for the party. ✦

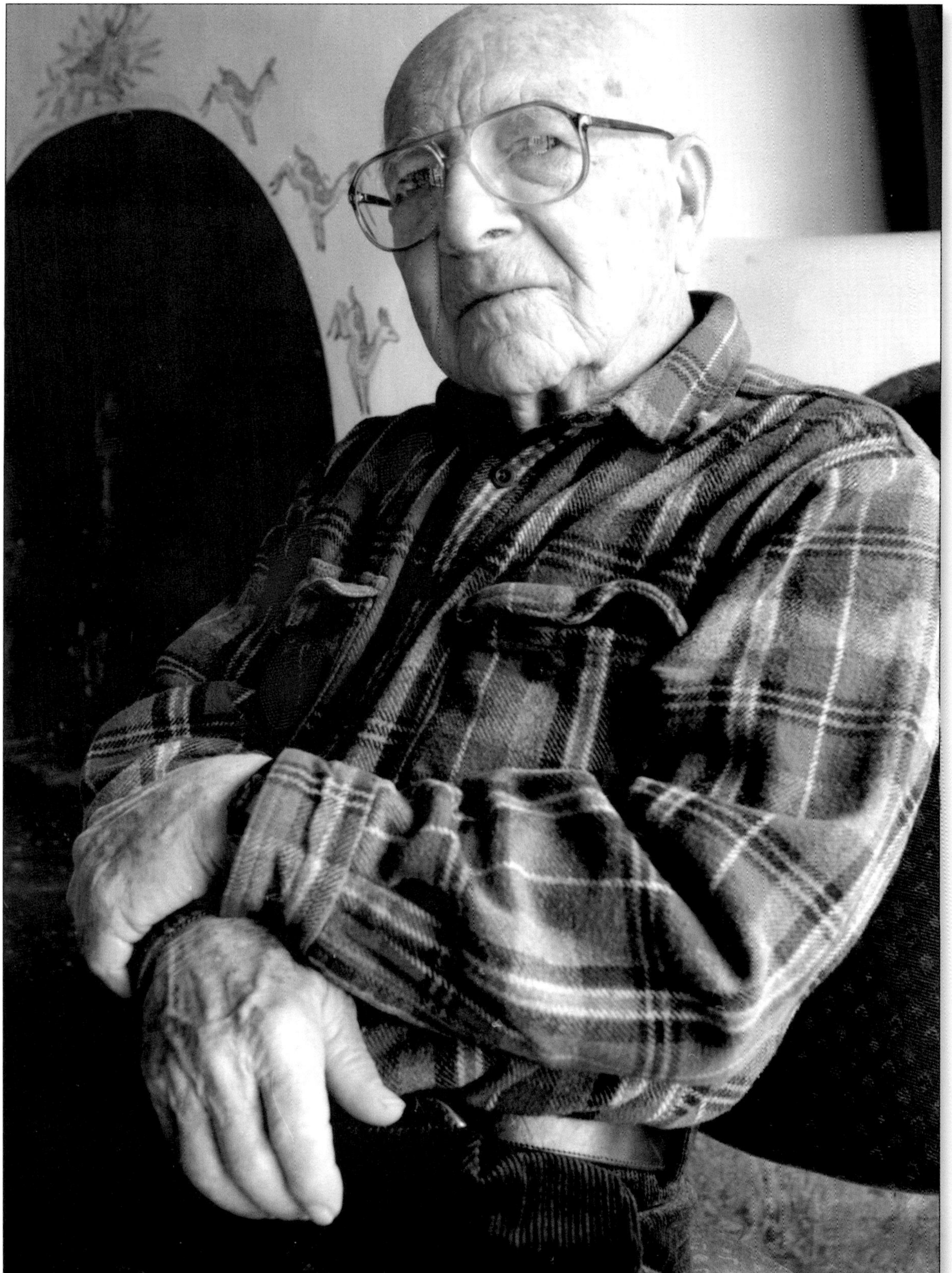

Consuelo "Connie" Fulgenzi

✦ Pass & Badge Office, worked July, 1945–1961

Connie Fulgenzi came to The Hill with five other young women from Las Vegas, New Mexico. In Las Vegas she had been a legal secretary, but she wanted to do something for the war effort since her husband, Larry, was serving on the battleship USS *Mississippi*.

"My first impression of Los Alamos was awful; I thought it looked like a mining camp," she said. "In fact, many of the girls I came up with left immediately, but I stuck it out."

"I lived in a dorm and I had my own room. I liked my job of helping people fill out the forms necessary for getting identification badges and then giving them the badges. I also liked the people on The Hill."

She went home to Las Vegas most weekends; but when she didn't go home, she attended the Saturday night dances.

"When I did learn they were working on an atom bomb, I was amazed. I knew they were working on something important. I was glad the war was over and Larry was coming home safely. He wouldn't be killed in the invasion of Japan."

"Larry later told me that when they sailed into Tokyo Harbor, it looked like there was snow on the terrain." He soon realized it could not have been snow. What he really saw were white flags of surrender on countless large guns that would have been fired at the U.S. invading troops." ✦

1944

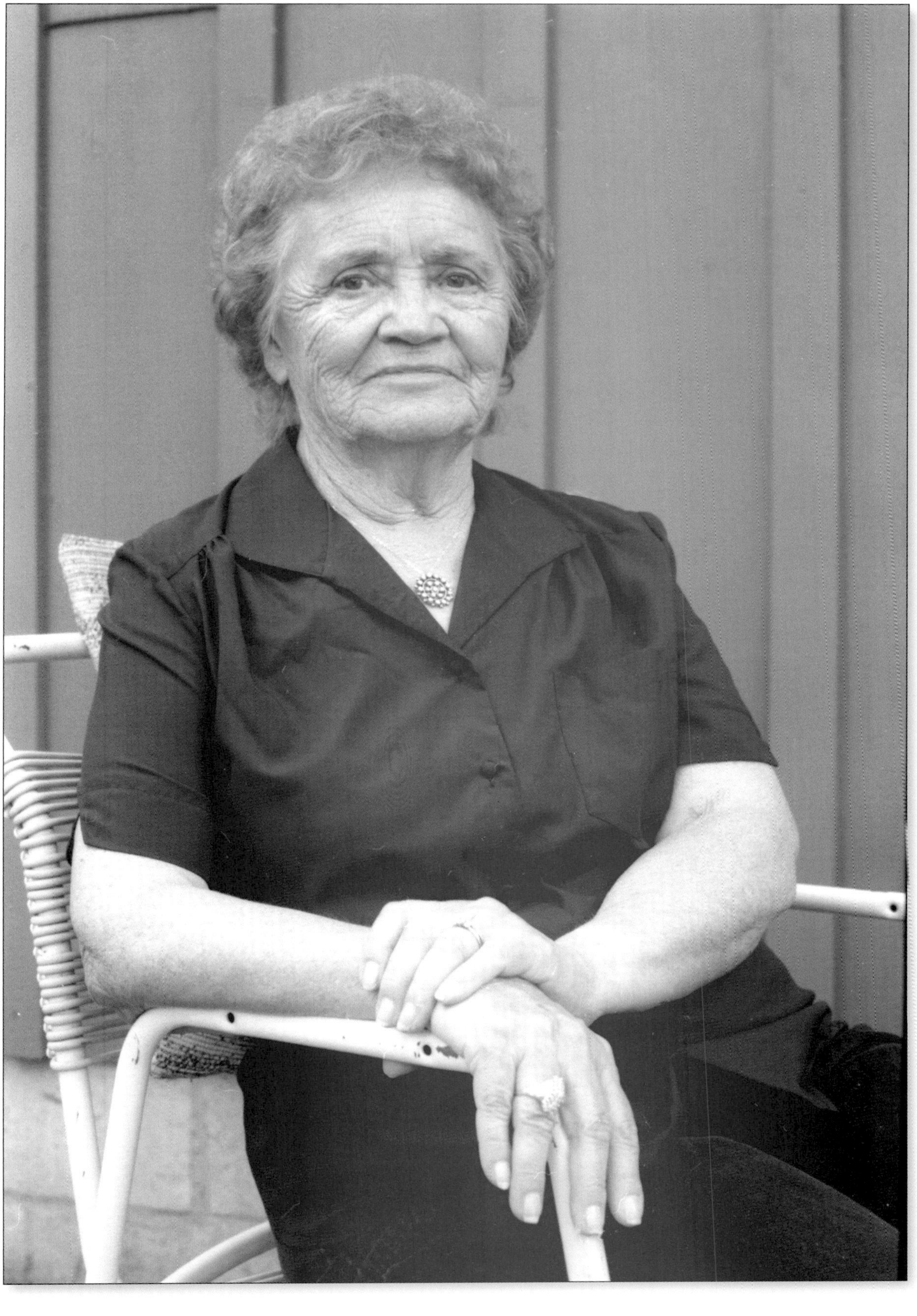

Carmen (Gallegos) Geoffrion

✦ Clerk/typist in Post Office, worked July, 1945–1961

"I have never been so homesick in my life as I was when I first came to Los Alamos." Gallegos' dad was an accountant on The Hill and he begged her not to come. "But being independent, I made the decision to come anyway."

"This was a dreary place," she recalls, "but I wasn't going to give up and go home to Las Vegas, New Mexico. I think I didn't want to give my dad the satisfaction of being right."

"It was always muddy at Los Alamos", she continued, "since it rained twice a day: once at noon and again at five in the evening."

Geoffrion said there was no address for Los Alamos as no one outside knew it existed. Instead there were post office-box numbers. Civilians used P.O. Box 1539, Lab people used P.O. Box 1663, and the Military Police used P.O. Box 1527. When babies were born, the post office box was used in place of a real address, and this caused much laughter on The Hill.

"When I asked what was being made here, the answer was 'We are building windshield wipers for submarines.' I really had no idea what was going on at Los Alamos until after the bomb went off at Hiroshima." ✦

1944

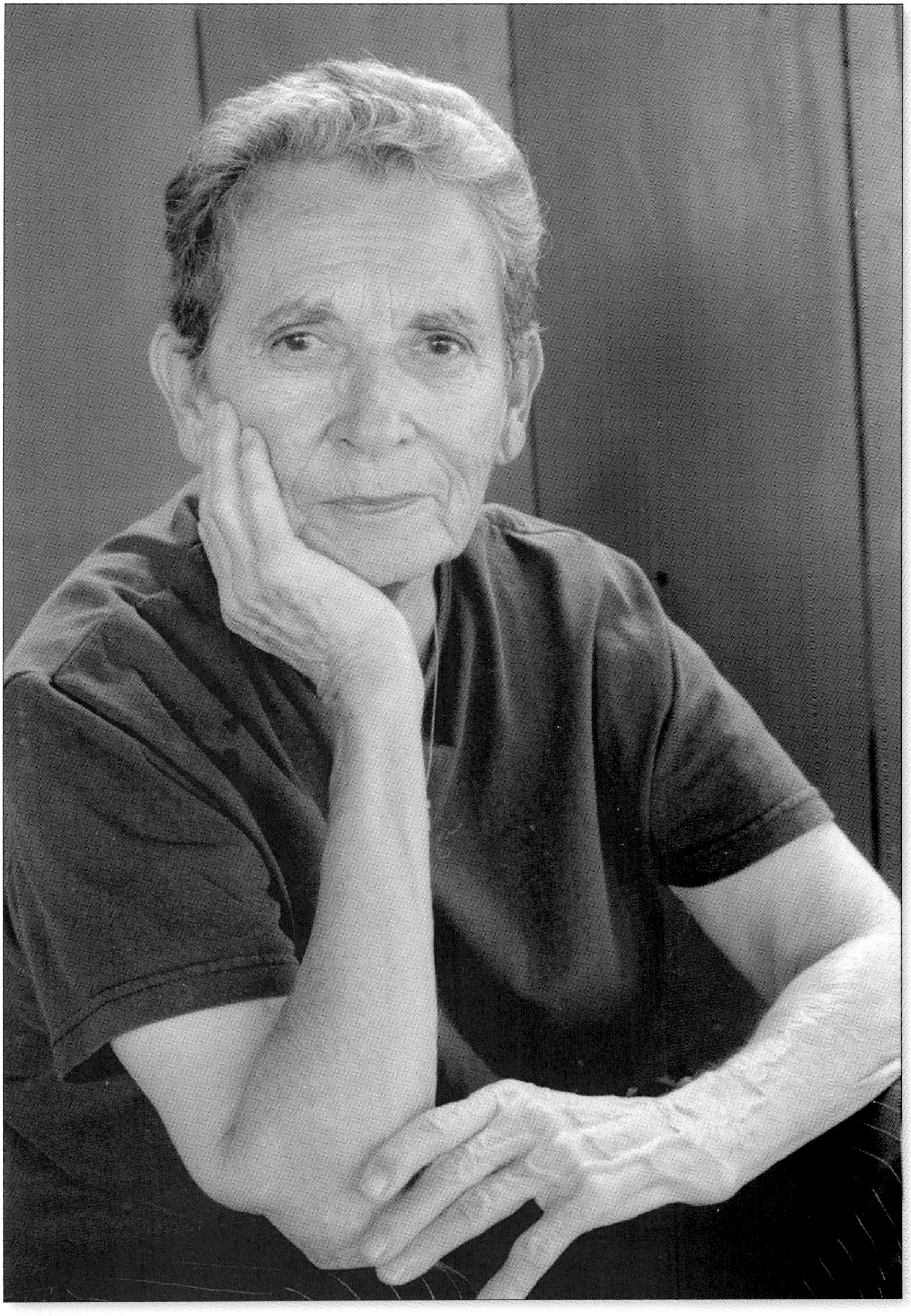

Severo Gonzales

+ Twelve-year-old son of Bences Gonzales, Commissary manager
+ Grew up in Los Alamos
+ Severo's grandfather was the original homesteader at Anchor Ranch which became a testing site

---

As a youngster, Severo Gonzales had a great opportunity to observe, as well as participate, in the day-to-day activities of life on The Hill. Before the government took over the Los Alamos Ranch School, Gonzales had worked there as houseboy. After the Project began he had other jobs. His dad ran the commissary that supplied foodstuffs to families, the PX, and the mess halls.

"I worked at the commissary in the meat department," he said. "I kept the long refrigerator meat trays clean, and also cleaned the meat grinder."

Gonzales remembers many of the occurrences in the commissary meat department. Everyone had a ration book; you could get items such as gasoline, coffee, tea, and meat *only* if you had enough ration stamps. The butchers, who were G.I.s, were always good-natured and friendly to the customers and sometimes they would offer a little extra help to the wives. They couldn't resist a lady begging to buy some meat when she did not have sufficient ration stamps. In return, the wives sometimes gave their benefactors small gifts to show their appreciation.

"One time I was given a present to give to the butcher. The gift was wrapped, so you could not see what it was. But I did peek into the bag—and what do you suppose it was? I was really surprised to see a bottle of whiskey."

Other fond memories are of his friendship with Kitty Oppenheimer. "My ten-year-old brother Victor took care of the Oppenheimers' horses. Many times I would go riding with Kitty in the western area where Los Alamos High School is located today."

The Oppenheimers owned two cars. Kitty would fill them up with gasoline, and as she hardly ever went anywhere, Gonzales said, she always had ration stamps left over. "I was just beginning to drive, and I always looked forward to Kitty's coming. I would drive her car around with her beside me and the other kids would see me." [Don't you know they were green with envy?]

Although the SEDs were not friendly to Gonzales, he notes, he was close to the MPs and the engineers. "Around the first of July, 1945, they mentioned to me that they would be gone for several days. I later learned that they had gone to Trinity Site for the atomic bomb test. I had suspected something—when I learned of the bomb, I wasn't too surprised. It was a very exciting time, and I am glad I was able to live there then." ✦

Katherine Oppenheimer
(Courtesy of Los Alamos National Lab Archives)

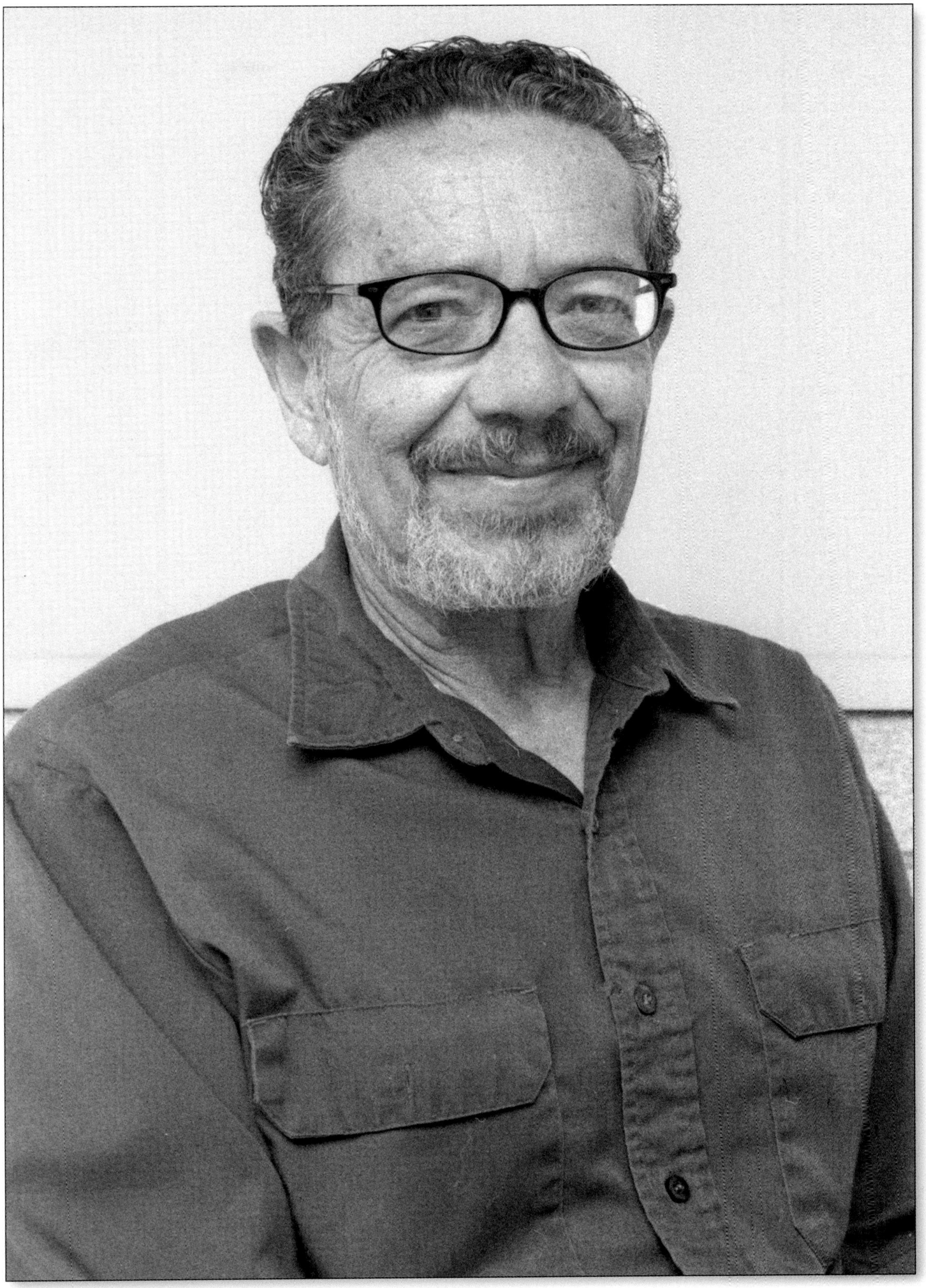

Arthur "Art" Hemmendinger, civilian

- Physicist, worked May, 1945–1977
- Measured the personal effects of induced radiation from neutrons
- Consultant for LANL afterwards

Arthur Hemmendinger was working at the Metallurgical Lab, University of Chicago, when the call went out that skilled machinists and physicists were needed in New Mexico. He decided to come to the Lab.

He said, "You could get housing if you were married, so I went out and got a wife. Then, I had written assurance that I would have a house."

"It was not an easy life in the early days of Los Alamos," Hennendinger reported. "When the coal furnace would back up, the baby's diapers would be covered in soot. We not only ran out of hot water but we ran out of water, period." Water was provided by the reservoir from the original Ranch School. (The school was taken over by the government for the Project.) When the water ran out, it had to be trucked in from the Rio Grande. Later wells were dug.

Of course there were no banks at Los Alamos, and workers could not bank in Santa Fe because of the secrecy. "We had to bank out of state." Shopping was almost non-existent. Some things could be bought in Santa Fe, but the Hemmendingers used the Sears catalog freely to buy what they needed.

"The Hill was permeated with a sense of urgency," Hemmendinger said. "We had to develop the atomic bomb before the Germans did." ✦

(Left to right), first row: **Norris Bradbury, John Manley, Enrico Fermi, Jerry Kellogg**; second row, **J.R. Oppenheimer, Dick Feynman**; third row, **Art Hemmindinger—over Oppie's shoulder** *(Courtesy of Los Alamos National Lab Archives)*

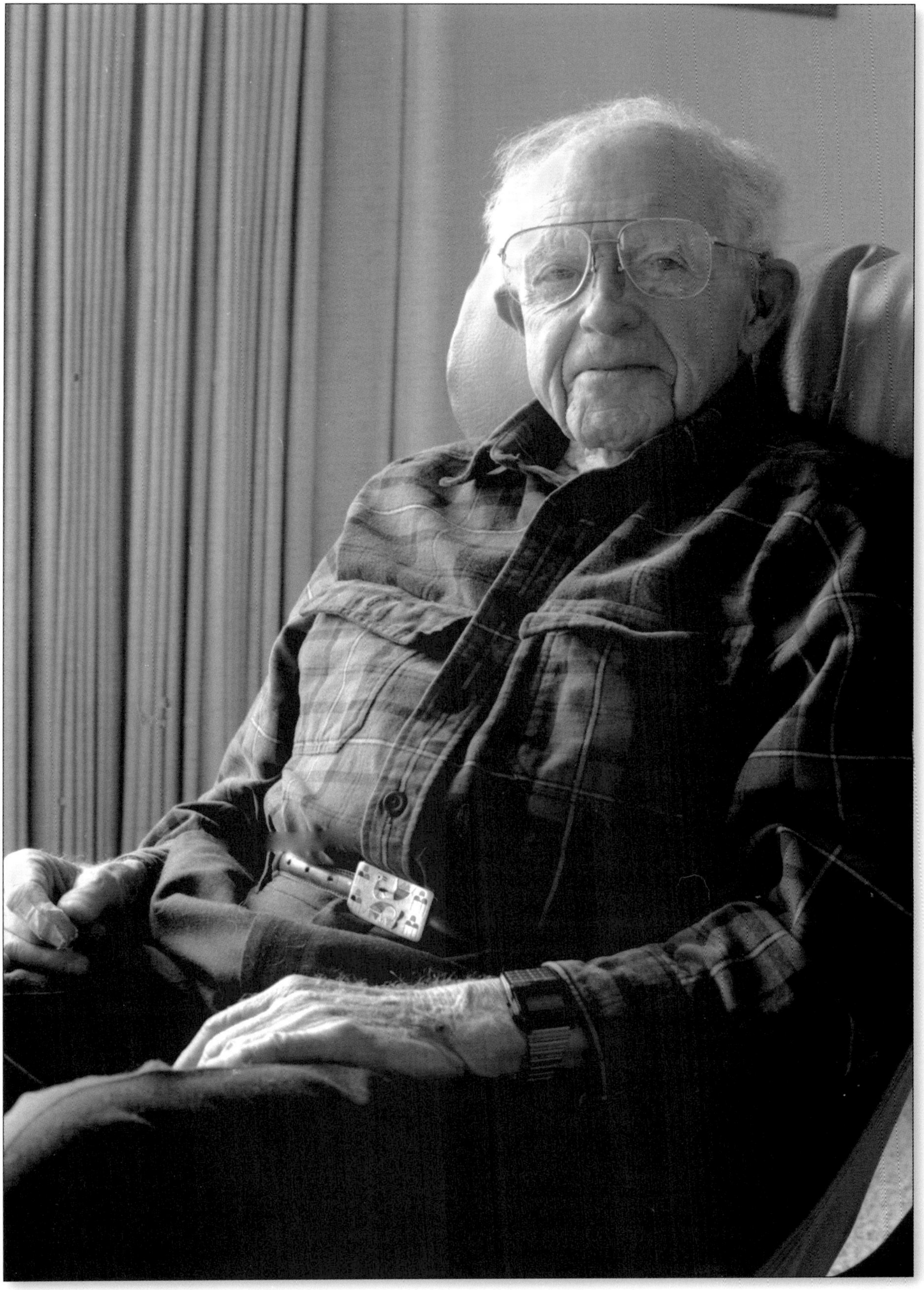

Peggy Hemmendinger

- ✦ Wife of Scientist Arthur Hemmendinger
- ✦ Lived on The Hill 1945–1977)

Peggy Hemmendinger came to Los Alamos as a bride of one week. Although she had bought items from Chicago's Marshall Field store, the items she would have needed as a new wife would not arrive in time. The pressure cooker she used was purchased from Sears Roebuck. She was lucky to get one of the only five that the company had received, as they were in short supply because of the war. Peggy was without even a pot in which to heat water, much less dishes and other kitchen necessities.

On their way up the unpaved track that served as a road to Los Alamos, the Hemmendingers stopped for an explosion test in progress. Here Arthur Hemmendinger encountered someone he already knew, Lyman Parratt, a physicist. A fortuitous meeting. Parratt and his wife Rhea were Mormon Church members, and it was through their efforts that the Hemmendingers were able to set up housekeeping.

"We existed on the kindness of the people from the Mormon Church. From their personal supplies they gave us dishes and pots and pans and whatever else we needed to survive until our things came. I don't know what we would have done without them. It wasn't as if we could have eaten at a restaurant *because there were none*."

The residents of Los Alamos had to be innovative, using whatever was at hand. "Arthur's books and records were shipped in sturdy wooden crates. When they came, he put shelves in the boxes, lacquered them with the same lacquer we used on our skis— and *voilà*, we had bookcases," noted Peggy.

"It was blue jeans by day and evening gowns at night," she went on. That was really a different experience for the young women. "There was an excitement generated by the people you were with; they were interesting and knowledgeable. Edward Teller, one of the scientists, was a fine pianist who owned a grand piano; sometimes he played for the guests at parties."

Complaints of improprieties in the dorms were brought to Oppenheimer. Some of the occupants of the single-sex dorms brought opposite-sex companions to spend the night. Nothing was done about the situation; Oppie said he would not monitor or interfere with adults.

Because of the large numbers of babies born during this time, an addition to the maternity wing of the hospital was added. General Groves was not pleased. "These blankety-blank people of Los Alamos are taking advantage of the U.S. government! But, I have a solution—we'll just shorten the lunch hour." That didn't happen. ✦

Peggy and Art Hemmindinger on left
(Courtesy of Los Alamos Historical Society Archives)

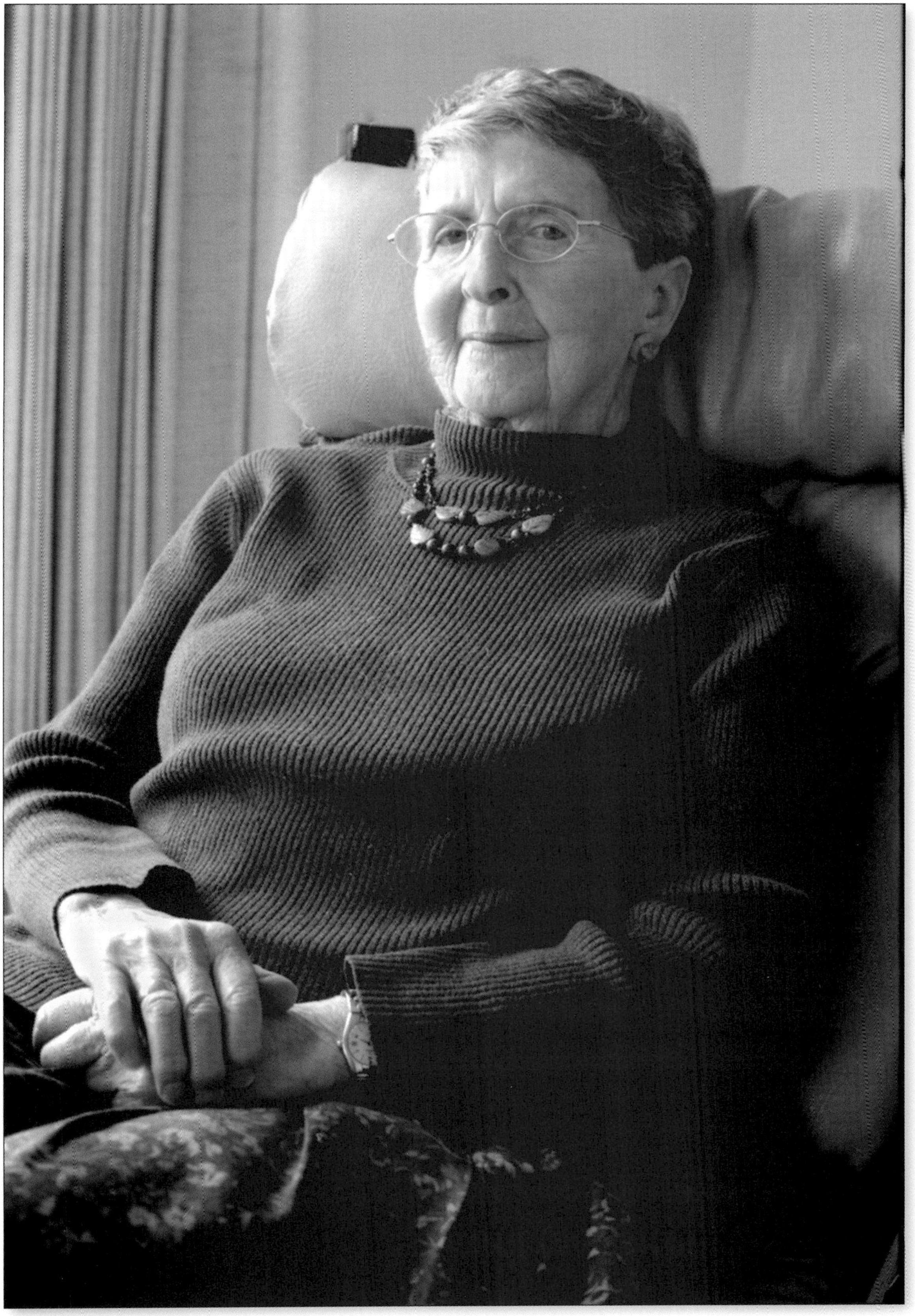

Carlton Hoogterp, civilian

- Physicist, worked September, 1943–September, 1977
- Critical assembly: put together Plutonium 235 into a ball with neutrons

One of the early scientists on The Hill, Carlton Hoogterp was recommended to Oppenheimer by Hoogterp's former college physics instructor at Southeast Missouri State College. That instructor was instrumental in seeing that Hoogterp went to Los Alamos.

He might not have thought himself fortunate to be at Los Alamos if he had been housed in a room on the second floor of his dormitory. Hoogterp remembers how lucky he felt the day a fire broke out in the dormitory. It demolished the second floor, but Hoogterp had a room downstairs which had no second floor above it. There was no damage to anything in his room. The fact that his room was undamaged did not matter in the end; all of the residents were evacuated to the barracks which weren't as comfortable as the dorm.

In July, 1945, Hoogterp was a member of the team that went to Trinity Site to set up for the atomic bomb test. "I was making blast-pressure measurements," he said. He remembers how hot and dry it was there. "I almost got sunburned," he noted.

After the successful test of the atomic bomb, Hoogterp and Bill Bright stayed to clean up some equipment. Finishing their work, they wanted what they considered an appropriate way to celebrate the success.

They couldn't think of anything much they could do. Their only option, they concluded, was to go to Albuquerque. There they spent the day getting drunk. (Weak beer was all that was available at Los Alamos unless you had your own private cache of hard liquor.)

Trinity Site was not the last place Hoogterp worked on bomb tests. After Trinity he flew to Bikini Island for more tests. "I feel that my work on the bomb was important, and I am proud to have been a part of the effort," he said. ✦

Carlton Hoogterp on his way to Bikini Island

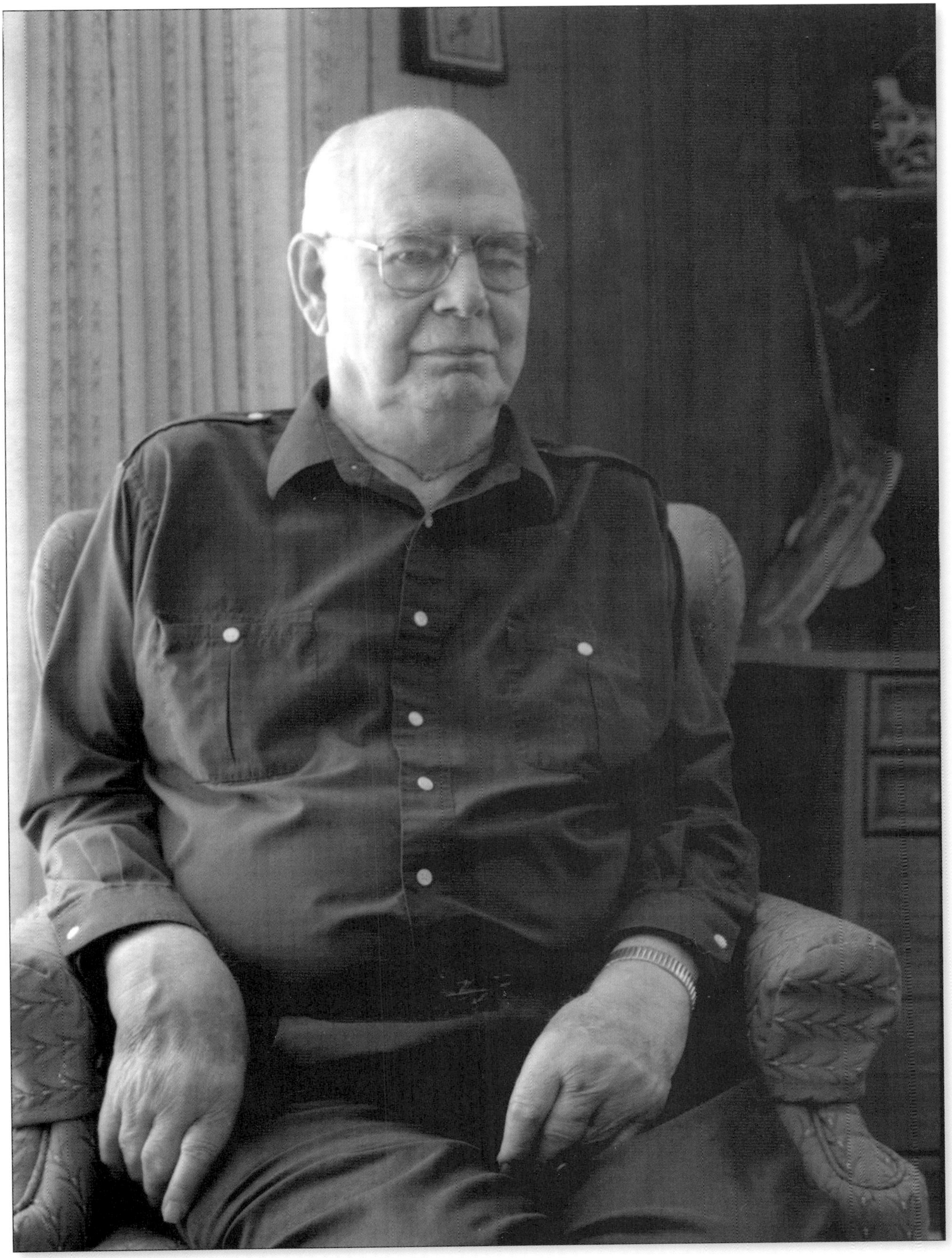

William "Bill" Hudgins, U.S. Army Tech Sergeant

- (SED) Special Engineer Detachment, August, 1943-1946
- Civilian employee 1946-September, 1984
- Chemistry/Metallurgy Area—Chemical analysis of polonium compounds

---

"No bureaucracy existed at Los Alamos during the war—that's why things got done, that's why the atomic bomb got built!" asserted Bill Hudgins. "Congress kept out of it; Groves (General Leslie R. Groves, Commanding Officer of the Manhattan Project) kept everyone out of it including the politicians and the bureaucrats." He went on to say that there were no forms to fill out to be "Okayed;" you just brought a picture and took it to the tool shops or to Carl Betz in the glass-blowing department. Then you got what you needed to complete your work.

In the tech area Betz stored his '32 Ford convertible with a rumble seat. He had bought it for $50, but it cost $500 to get it to The Hill. "We were encouraged to use all of the Lab facilities (this was supposed to keep us occupied and happy), so I had access to a lot of non-classified materials. We used five gallons of paint remover on that car. It ended up having twenty-four coats of lacquer, new tires, new upholstery, and it even received new chrome plating. Looked like a brand-new car."

Hudgins says he used to tool around with Betz in the car on the back roads after work. Security patrolled the roads with a tank, he added.

One day when they were wandering around in the canyons, they got lost. Then they found a crossover road that led to an old abandoned homestead built in the 1920s. The people had probably been dry farmers who were there only in the summer and had a permanent residence in the valley, Hudgins noted. The homestead included a barn, a corral, and a chicken coop. The house, built of square logs, consisted of two rooms with space in the middle for a wagon.

"I was entranced by the scene," noted Hudgins. "I was a city boy and had never seen or envisioned anything like this before."

Later, he said, he returned, only to find the buildings bulldozed to make way for a cemetery. "It was sad to see that old homestead and its buildings gone; it's like a part of the history of the area was just obliterated," he ended. ✦

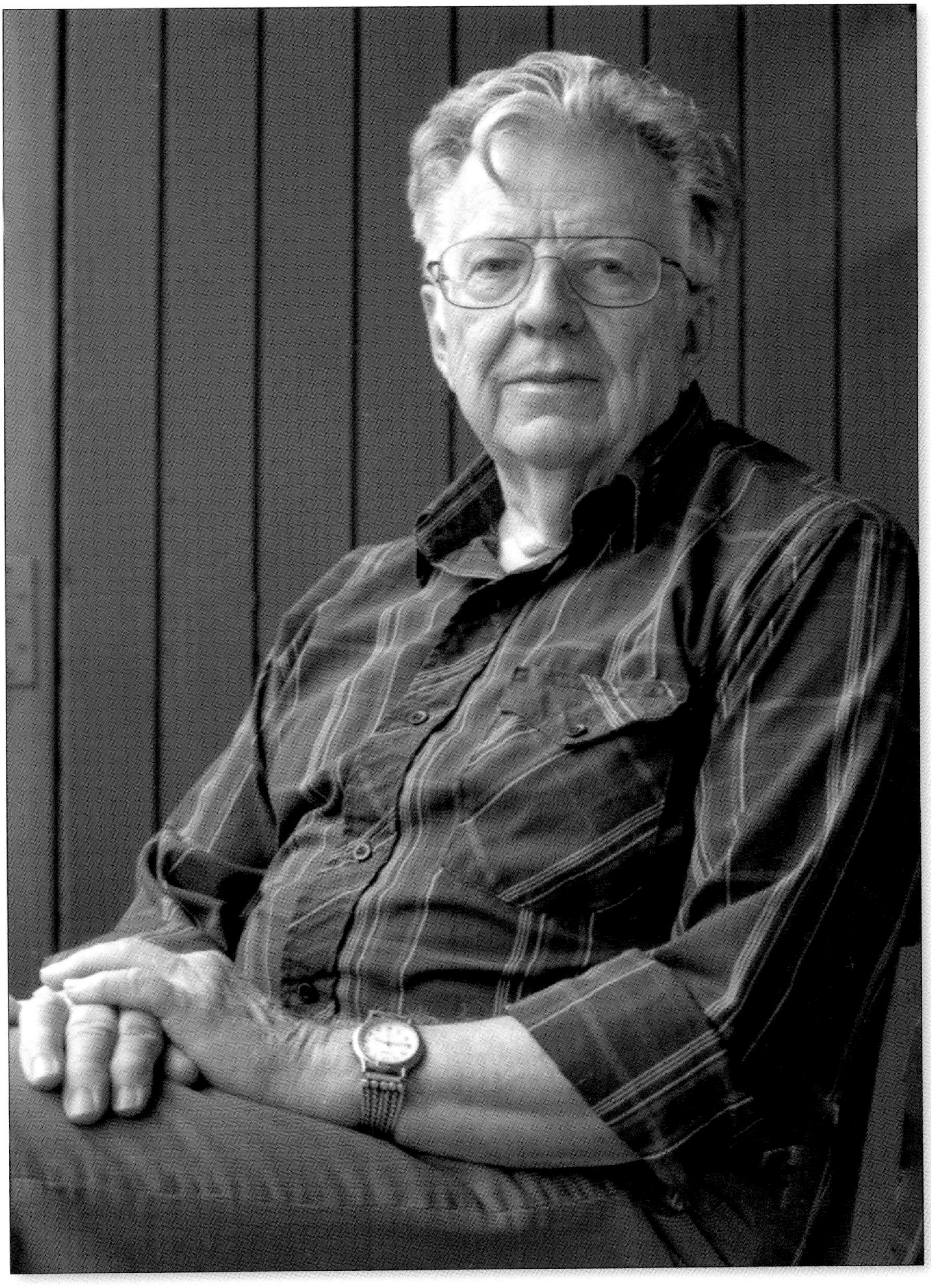

Gordon Knobeloch, U.S. Army

✦ (SED) Special Engineer Detachment, January, 1945–1946
✦ Civilian employee 1951–1987
✦ RALA Group (radioactive lanthanum)—Chemist working with implosion

---

When Gordon Knobeloch stepped off the train during its brief stop at Lamy, New Mexico, he was certain he was at the wrong place. This didn't look like *anything*. using a crank phone [can you imagine?] he called Dorothy McKibbin at 109 E. Palace Ave., and he was soon picked up and driven up to The Hill.

Working with the RALA group, Knobeloch needed a device that would grind wood into little pieces to be used in the diagnostic testing of bombs, so he and Rene Prestwood went into Santa Fe to find a garbage disposer. He was certain that was certain to do the job. However he couldn't tell the sales person why he needed the disposer. The salesman was perplexed when Knobeloch inquired as to whether or not the grinder would work without water. The men could not, of course, reveal why they needed to use it in that manner. When the salesman told them it would not operate well without water, they abandoned the whole idea and left without the disposer.

In addition to working with the RALA group, Knobeloch collaborated with eight or ten of the physicists. "The implosion experiment was the single most important experiment affecting the final design of the atomic bomb," Knobeloch emphasized.

When Gordon retired, he let his security clearance lapse, as did most retiring scientists. He had absolutely no need for it anymore. About ten years later Knobeloch received a call from someone at the Lab who was interested in Knobeloch's work during the war. He asked if Knobeloch would agree to come to the Lab and be videotaped discussing his work on the bomb. Gordon agreed to come in, and the two men set a morning videotaping appointment.

The day came and Knobeloch obligingly showed up at the appointed time and place. He spent the whole morning recounting his work on the bomb. Finally, the history was complete and he could breathe a sigh of relief. Suddenly he had another thought: *what if he had made an error in what he said* or *had forgotten an important detail*.

I'd like to review the tape, he requested of his videographer. "Oh," responded the videographer, "you can't look at the tape. It's classified!" ✦

Gordon Knobeloch, left, and buddies

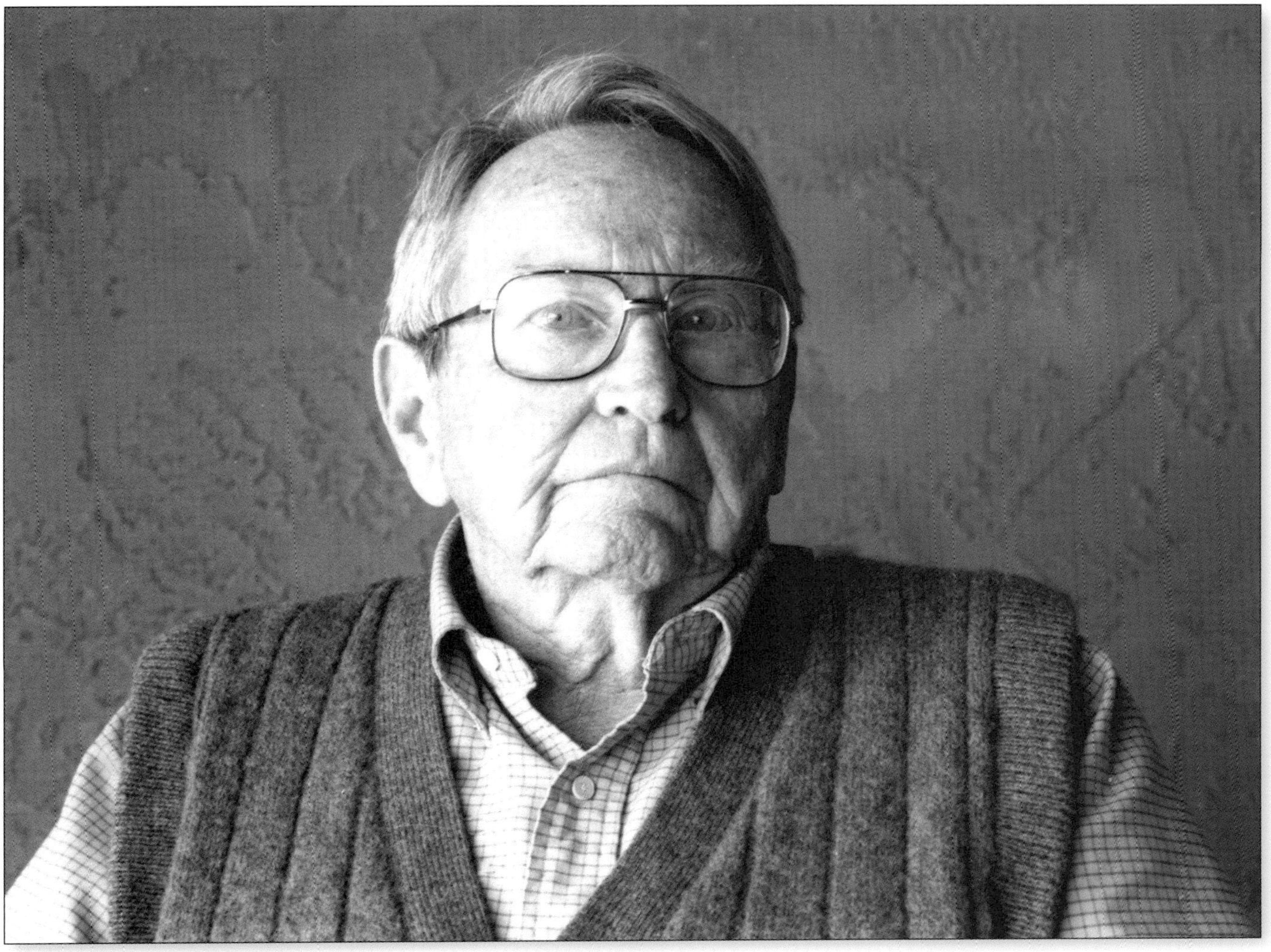

Katherine "Pat" (Patterson) Krikorian

- ✦ (WAC) U.S. Women's Army Corps, August, 1943–1945
- ✦ Secretary

When Pat Patterson asked to go overseas, she never expected go to The Hill instead, but she was among the first twenty-five WACs sent to Los Alamos.

She recollected the very cold winter of 1943–44 when The Hill experienced an early freeze and a twenty-one-inch snowstorm—in September.

She and two WAC friends worked at the multi-purpose movie "theater" that also housed church services on Sundays, Saturday-night dances, and other functions. The movie let out about 10 pm and Pat, Martha Ann Talley, and Jo Julius began their trek back to their dormitory.

Because it was so cold, they decided to take a shortcut near the now-frozen Ashley Pond (named for a man called Ashley Pond). Near the edge of the pond they came upon four ducks, frozen immobile in the ice. The WACs couldn't just leave them there; but what should they do? Being resourceful people, they headed to the fire station for help. There they borrowed a hatchet and tramped back to the sitting ducks. They chopped the ice from around the ducks one by one, carried them back to the fire station, and put them under a big pot-bellied stove which had a blazing fire in it, and waited...

Pat Krikorian, second from left.

About thirty minutes later, the ducks showed signs of life and tried to end their captivity. They let out nary a quack, however. Once Pat, Martha Ann, and Jo saw that the ducks would recover, the girls ran for their dorm—bed check was at eleven. That was the last time ducks were left to winter at Los Alamos; they were brought to warmer areas in the fall. Lucky ducks... ✦

78

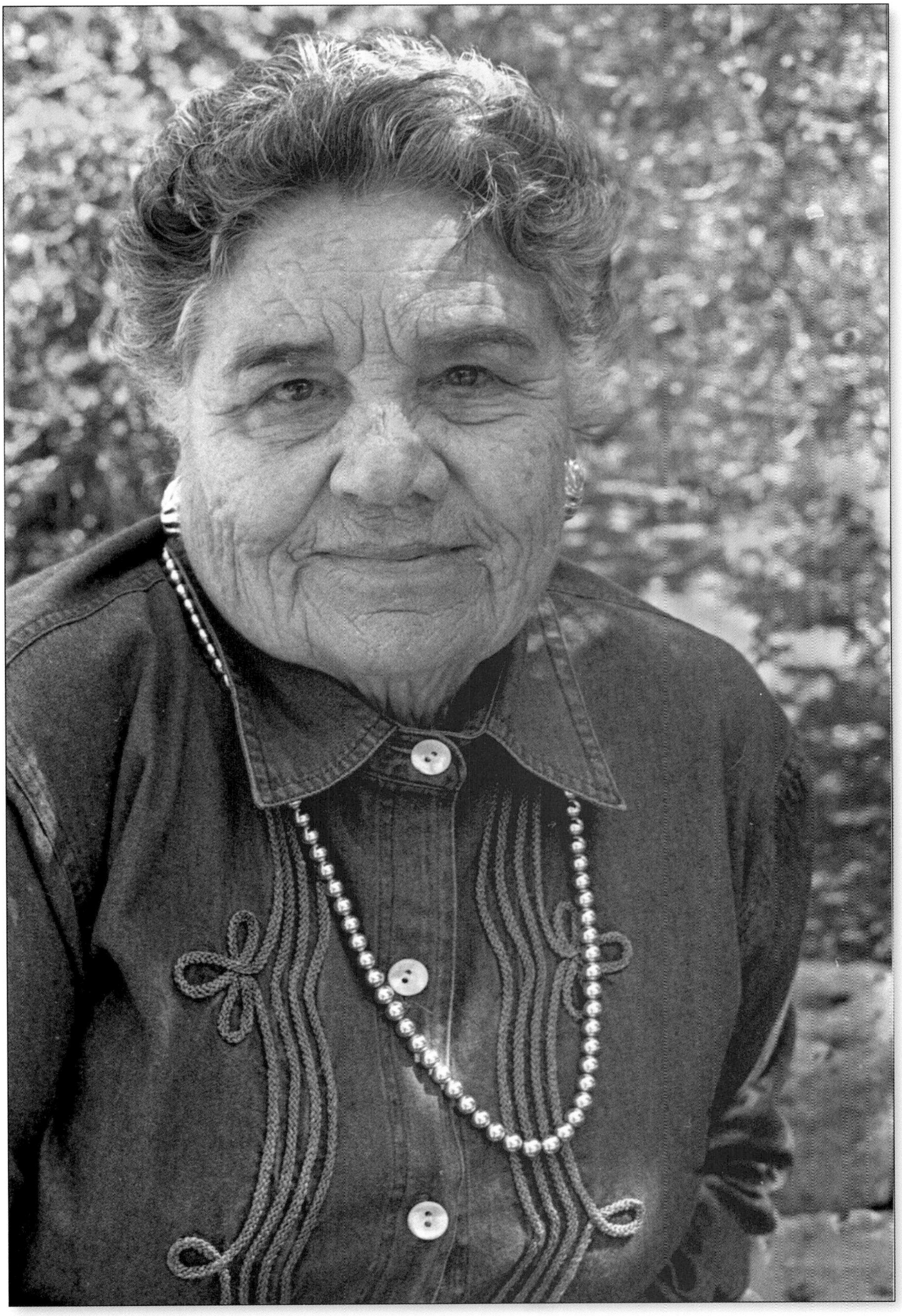

Joseph "Joe" Leary, U.S. Army

- ✦ (SED) Special Engineer Detachment, November, 1944–1946
- ✦ Civilian employee 1946–1974
- ✦ Chemical engineer, physical chemist—Processed lanthanum for implosion testing

Joe Leary worked with the RALA group (radioactive lanthium) processing lanthium for the weekly implosion testings. His most memorable experience involved his work with RALA.

"I usually rode down to Bayo Canyon with Ken Walsh, who worked with me on the project, where the testing was set up. Because of the contamination from the explosions we had to shower and change clothes right after working on the site. Of course security was always tight, and we had to leave through the MP gate."

It so happened, Leary continued, that some trinitite fused with green sand from the first atomic bomb test was stolen from the Lab. The MPs had been given a counter of radioactivity so they could check everyone who came through their gate for radioactivity from the stolen trinitite. On this occasion, Leary and Walsh finished their work at the site and proceeded to drive through the MP gate. "Stop," the MPs instructed, "and get out of the car." The detector had registered radioactivity. The car was searched for trinitite; then the two men were searched. No trinitite was found, but the men were not allowed to go because the counter was still registering activity.

The RALA group: Joe Leary is in last row, second from right.

Leary had an idea: "Just let us walk fifty feet up the road and see if the counter changes." The counter showed less activity. The MPs didn't know what to do. This situation was unusual, so they called their captain and asked him what to do.

"Where do they work?" asked the captain. "Bayo Canyon," answered the MP.

"Well, let them go and just tell them to go home." ✦

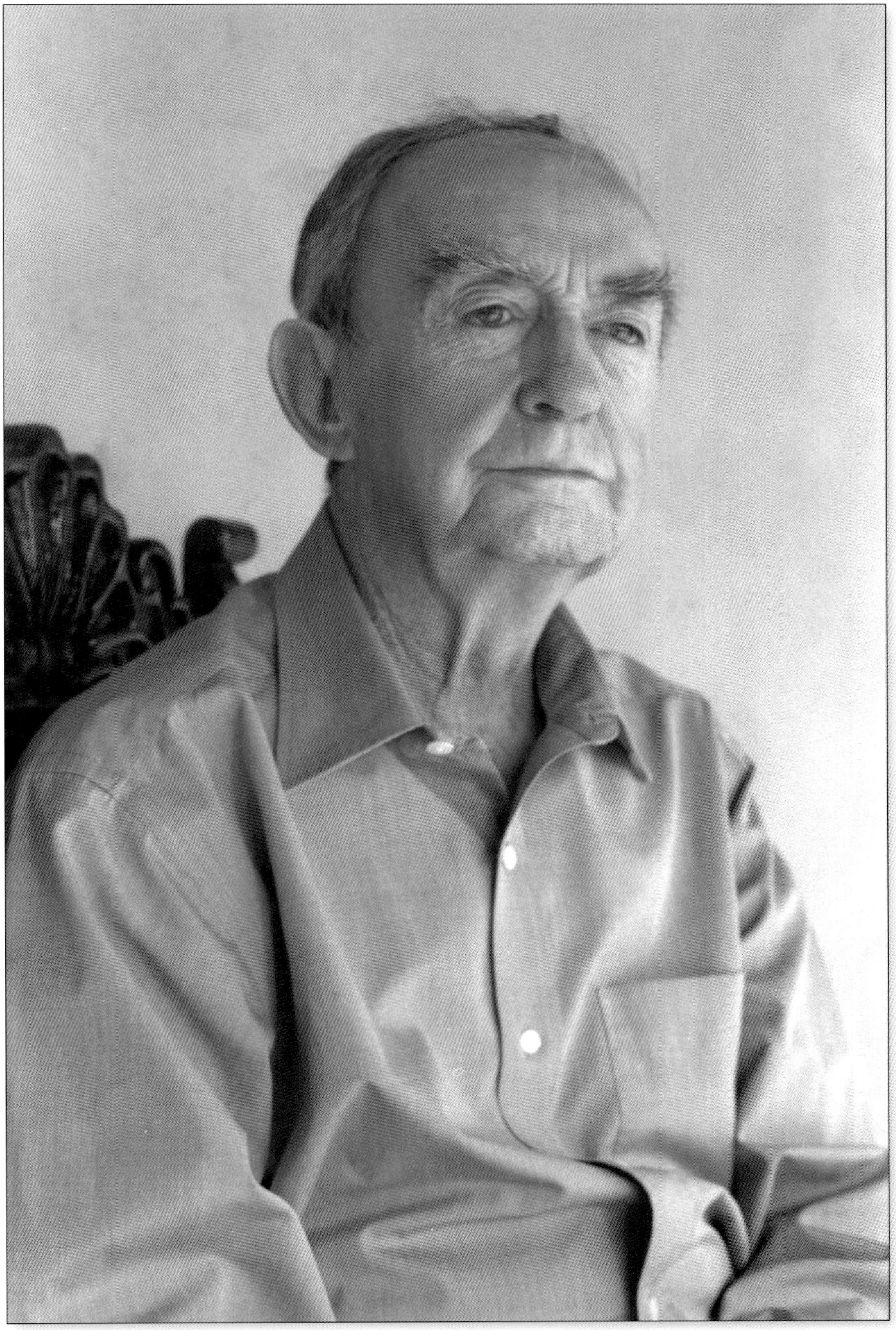

Kathleen "Kay" Mark

✦ Wife of Scientist J. Carson Mark, director of Theoretical Division
✦ Lived on The Hill July, 1945–September, 2004

When Kay Mark heard what Los Alamos was like, she thought it must be a funny place. Her husband described it as a location with a wonderful climate: clouds, rain, and hail, followed by a burst of sunlight. "I couldn't imagine what that was like," she said. She had never experienced a climate like that.

The Marks' were Canadians. Kay came by train, bringing her three children and her six-week-old baby in a clothes basket. Her husband, Carson, a mathematician, was already at Los Alamos, working on the atomic bomb.

She remembered that construction was always going on at Los Alamos. "One time, the men were digging a large ditch with a giant machine. My children were curious and went over to watch the work. My three-year-old got too close to the edge and fell in. It was quite a job to get him out amid all of the commotion and crying and screaming that went on," she said.

The Marks' hosted many social gatherings at their home. Guests included many of the Lab's most important scientists. Kay was known to her guests for her English plum pudding at Christmas time.

She was interested in geology and attended the University of New Mexico, taking many classes, and, she authored several books about geology. She was also involved in public education in Los Alamos, working to improve the schools there.

The Marks had a total of six children, all of whom grew up in Los Alamos. ✦

Kay Mark with Elizabeth, Joan, Graham and Tom
(Courtesy of Los Alamos Historical Society Archives)

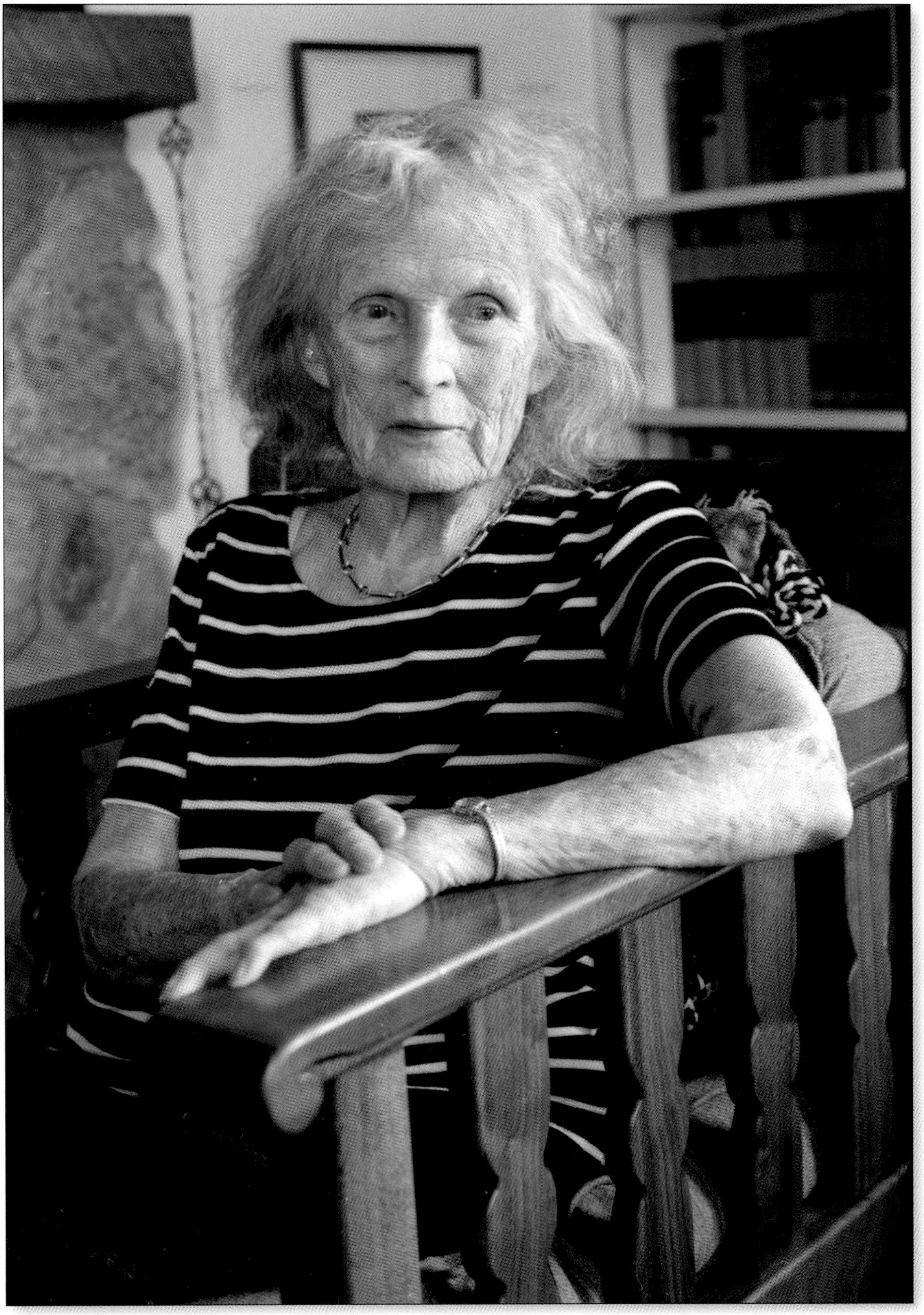

Angelita (Vigil) Martinez

✦ Potter Maria Martinez's niece by marriage, worked 1943–1946
✦ Housekeeping and child care

Angelita Martinez was the housekeeping teacher for many young wives on The Hill: she taught them how to clean and take care of a home. "They were young girls who didn't know about cleaning and didn't even have a broom or dustpan or Dutch Cleanser," said Martinez. "Also I was the one who decided when we needed to wash clothes, so I was in charge of the laundry too." For these services, she received $2.50 a day—she brought her own lunch from home.

Alhough Angelita was ninety-seven years old at the time of this interview, the memories of the square dancing on Friday and Saturday nights had not faded. "We took turns as to where the dances were to be held; sometimes at Fuller Lodge on The Hill, and sometimes down here at San Ildefonso Pueblo. There were no glass windows here at the Pueblo and we had to put blankets over the openings. To heat the room, we would light up a big pot-bellied stove."

Martinez noted that Norris Bradbury, "Oppie," and Edward Teller were among the notables attending the dances. She said that the elderly came too.

It wasn't strictly square dancing either. "We taught them Indian dances, and we learned western dances and the two-step." Because there was little recreation at Los Alamos, everyone looked forward to going to these dances. Also, those who attended could enjoy the homemade pies and cookies.

Angelita's husband, Miguel Martinez, was the singer and drummer for the dances. "The ladies liked him and enjoyed dancing with him," she said. "A good time was had by all despite the hardships, which included muddy streets, and sometimes a shortage of water," she concluded. ✦

Angelita Martinez on left

Traditional braided belt dance
(Courtesy of Los Alamos National Lab Archives)

Traditional dance demonstration, Norris and Lois Bradbury in background at left
(Courtesy of Los Alamos National Lab Archives)

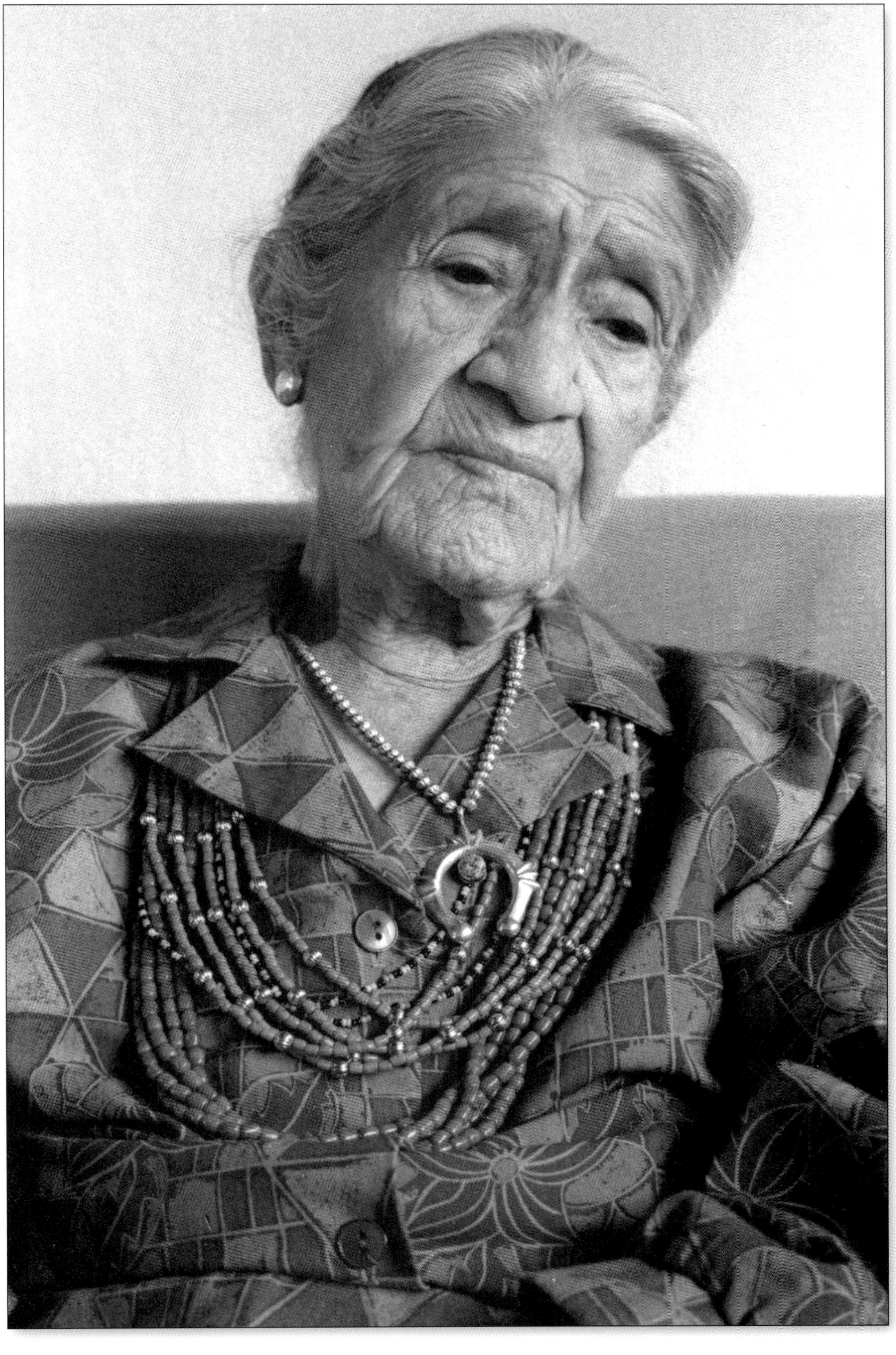

John Mench, U.S. Army

- ✦ (SED) Special Engineer Detachment, October, 1943–1946
- ✦ Foundry engineer, made bomb casings during the war
- ✦ Civilian Employee 1946–July, 1977

John Mench started the Los Alamos Little Theater that still flourishes today with the leadership of seven other enthusiasts. In fact, it is the oldest organization in Los Alamos other than the Lab itself.

Mench was always looking for people to act in the theater's productions. One day he asked Oppenheimer if he would be in one of the plays. "Well," said Oppie, "I will be in a production as long as I don't have to memorize lines or attend rehearsals."

Mench thought and thought and researched plays which would fit the parameters. And, Mench found just the perfect role for Oppie, one that fit Oppenheimer's specifications exactly: Oppie became the corpse in *Arsenic and Old Lace*.

Many at Los Alamos went to the dances. Those were the days of jitterbugging and dancing to music like that of Glenn Miller. At one of those dances, Mench met a WAC who liked to dance too. They really had a good time.

One day she invited him to Sunday lunch at the WAC Mess Hall where, he noted, the fare was heavenly in contrast to the mess hall where the soldiers and civilians normally ate. He was delighted to go, and accepted with enthusiasm, relishing the thought of great food.

He reported that although he enjoyed the lunch a lot, he thinks perhaps his companion did not enjoy it nearly as much. Mench spent the entire time with his WAC hostess talking about his wife, who was back home and whom he missed very much. (Soldiers' wives were not allowed on The Hill.)

"For some reason," Mench said, "she never invited me again." ✦

J. Robert Oppenheimer
(Courtesy of Los Alamos Historical Society Archives)

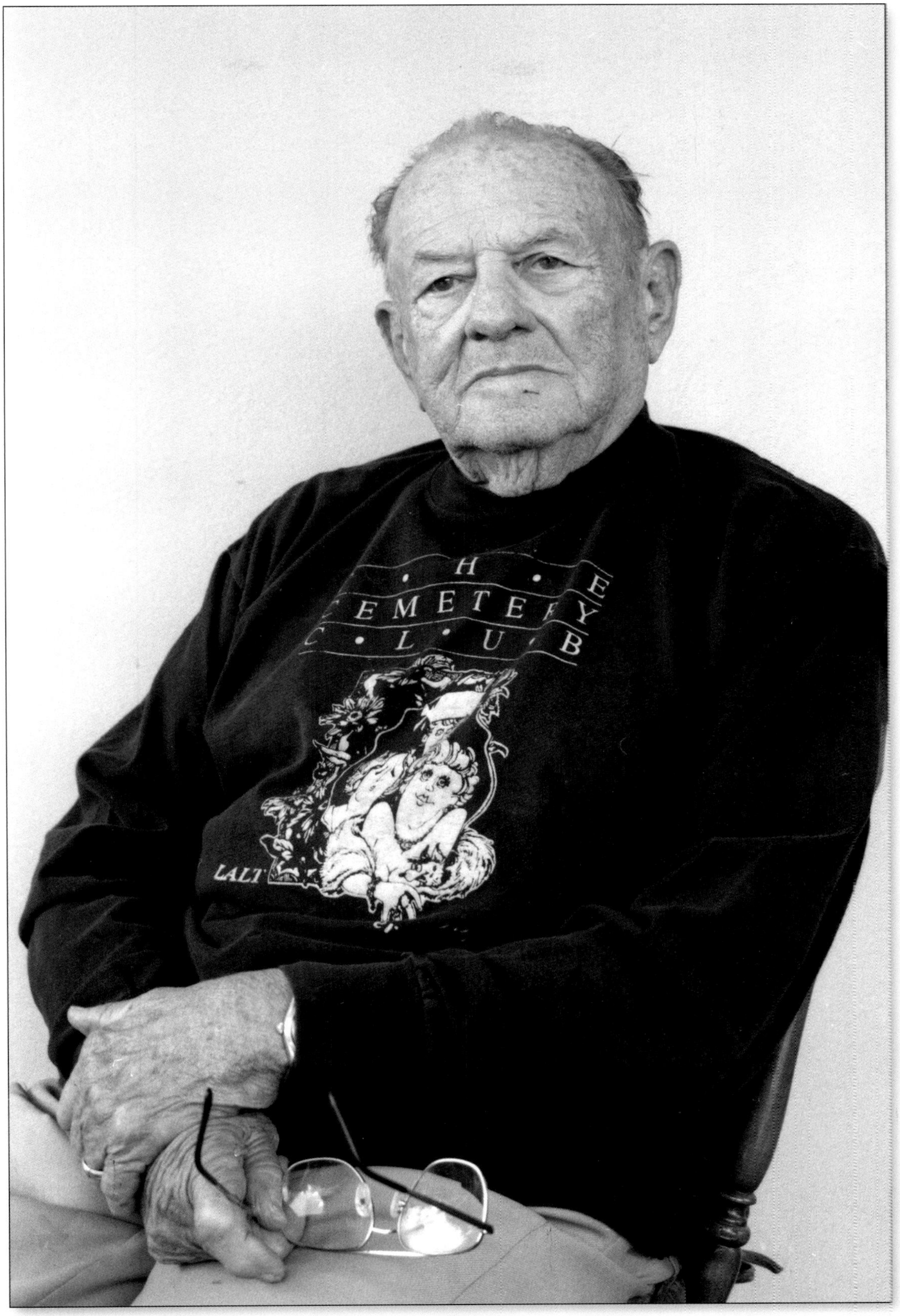
C · L · U · B

Roy G. Merryman, U.S. Army

- ✦ (SED) Special Engineering Detachment, December, 1944–1946
- ✦ Civilian employee 1946–1982
- ✦ Chemical engineer, Chemistry/Metallurgy Division—Coordinator of design elements

Roy Merryman used his design talents in creative ways. In the machine shop he fashioned lucite tables and lab furniture among other items, but his biggest project came a little later.

One of the men had a fourteen-foot motorboat parked in the tech area. Merryman and several others were recruited to design items for the boat including seats, a rudder, and a mast. He also made a sail for the mast out of silk. All of these items came from unused scrap material from the Lab.

When these tasks were completed, the boat was ready for its maiden voyage. Five men accompanied the boat to El Vado Lake, where they set sail. As the boat neared the middle of the lake, they noticed big ominous-looking clouds forming as the wind picked up.

Whoops! First the mast blew over; then the boat tilted. *Merryman could not swim*; the others could. "I made peace with my maker," he recalls, "but, finally, the boat righted itself and I lived to tell the tale. We paddled her back to shore."

"I learned to swim at fifty-five, and I am now a certified Red Cross swim instructor." ✦

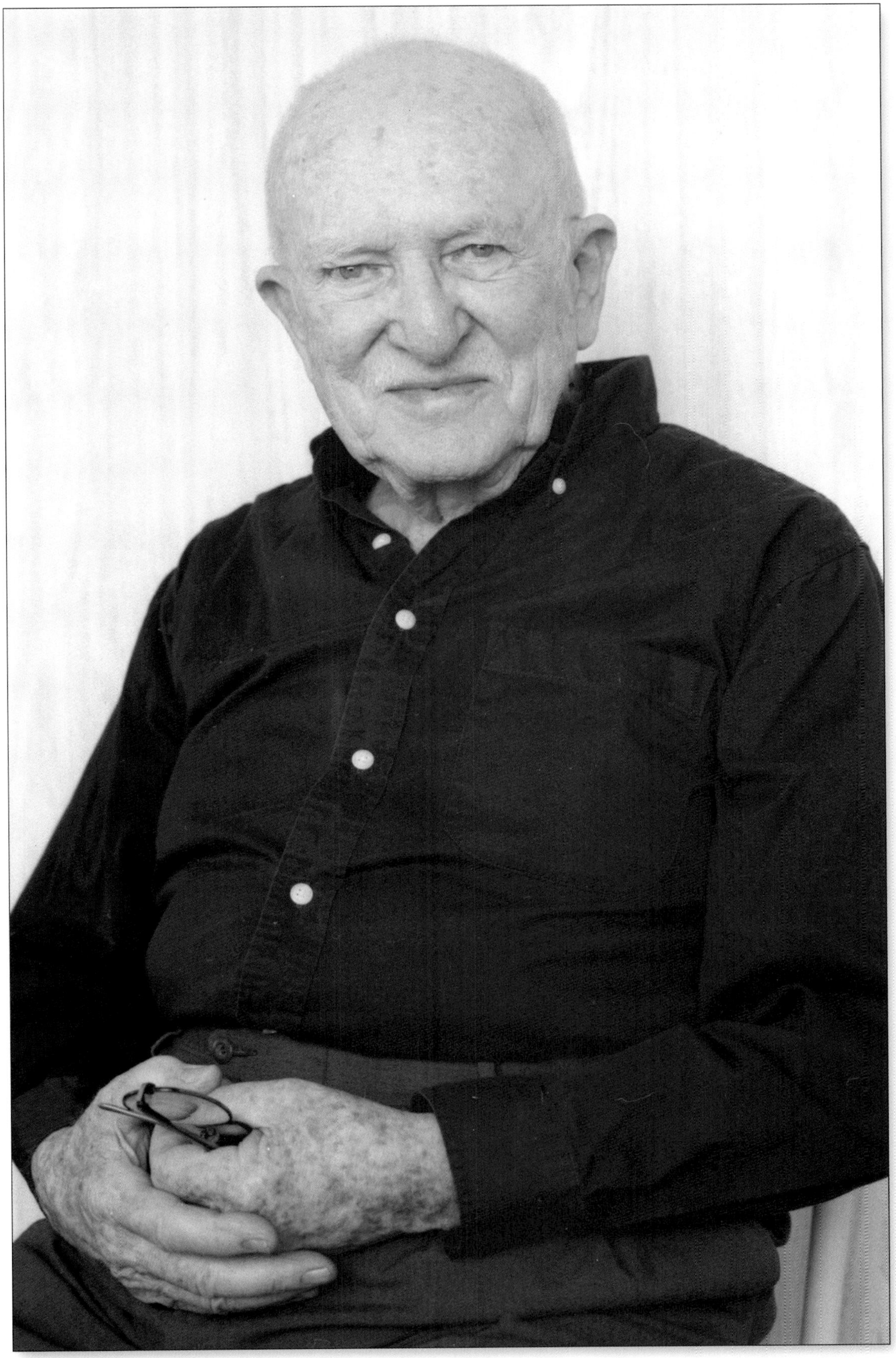

John "Mike" Michnovicz, U.S. Army Tech Sergeant

- ✦ (SED) Special Engineer Detachment, October, 1944-1946
- ✦ Civilian employee 1946-1948
- ✦ Sandia Labs 1948-1988—Photographer

When Mike Michnovicz came to the Manhattan Project, he assumed he was going to use his background in electrical engineering and physics. But officials found that he also had a lot of experience in photography, so that is what he did. He photographed many of the top Project scientists and had other assignments including documentary shots, and photos of technical drawings.

After the successful test of the atomic bomb, there was a need for a good photographic portrait of Oppenheimer. Michnovicz was given the assignment. He set up big flood lamps for the sitting. Then, Michnovicz recalls, he learned that he had only ten minutes to take the photograph. Using 8x10 sheet film, there was only time for four or five shots. That photograph has been used all over the world.

Another of Michnivicz's accomplishments was his photograph for the Enrico Fermi Medal. The medal was given for outstanding achievement. (Fermi was one of the leading Manhattan Project scientists.) Michnivicz's photograph of Fermi was used for the medal.

Since Michnovicz was also a very good accordionist. he was much in demand for dances and parties. He also was part of a musical group called Los Quatros, made up of four musicians who played accordion, violin, guitar, and bass.

On The Hill, Michnovicz met three attractive young women from Las Vegas, Nevada. He said to one of his buddies, "I am going to marry one of those girls."

And he did. He married Mary Louise Maloney. ✦

Los Quatros, Mike on left

Mary Lou Maloney and Mike Michnovicz

90

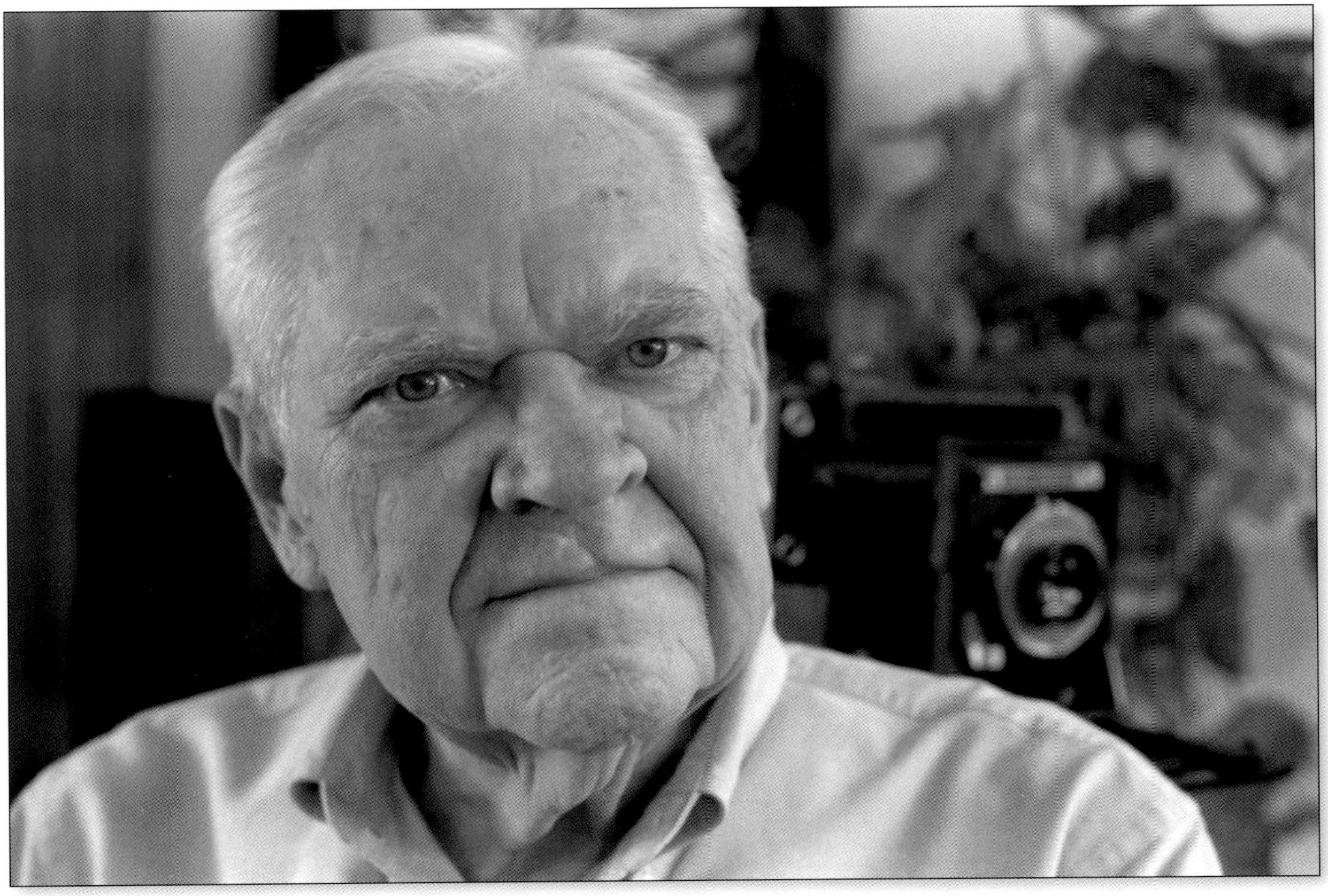

Mary Louise (Maloney) Michnovicz

✦ Clerk/Typist, worked June, 1945–July, 1948

Mary Lou Maloney came to The Hill from Las Vegas, New Mexico. She previously had a job in Las Vegas at Camp Luna with the U.S. Air Transport Command. Then she had the opportunity to get a different job. The recruiter hired all of the women in Las Vegas who applied.

"I was off to the biggest adventure of my life up to that point, as I was only eighteen years old at the time. I couldn't get over the fact that there was mud everywhere I looked. And to top it all off, there were three gates manned by mean-looking MPs."

Maloney's first "big adventure" came when she was brought to her new lodging, a dorm room which housed two women. Her room was on the ground floor. Imagine her shock when she saw workmen staring through the windows at her on that first morning. "I was furious," she related. "One of the first things I did after that was make curtains for the windows."

At first, she worked at the commissary, but eventually she worked in an office. "I was really having a good time being on The Hill," she noted.

"I met Mike Michnovicz at a Valentine dance. Connie Meyer, Marie Frank, and I were a singing trio at the dance. I was not looking for a serious boyfriend; I was just having fun," she insisted. Mary Lou went on to say she had noticed Mike before then—had seen him around.

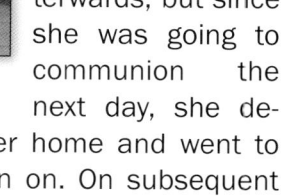

He asked to take her to get something to eat afterwards, but since she was going to communion the next day, she demurred. Mike did walk her home and went to church with her from then on. On subsequent dates, they often went to La Fonda Hotel in Santa Fe to eat.

Michnovicz ended, "I am proud of contributing to the development of the bomb. I am just glad we [the United States] did it and not someone else." ✦

Mary Lou Maloney and Mike Michnovicz

Singing Trio

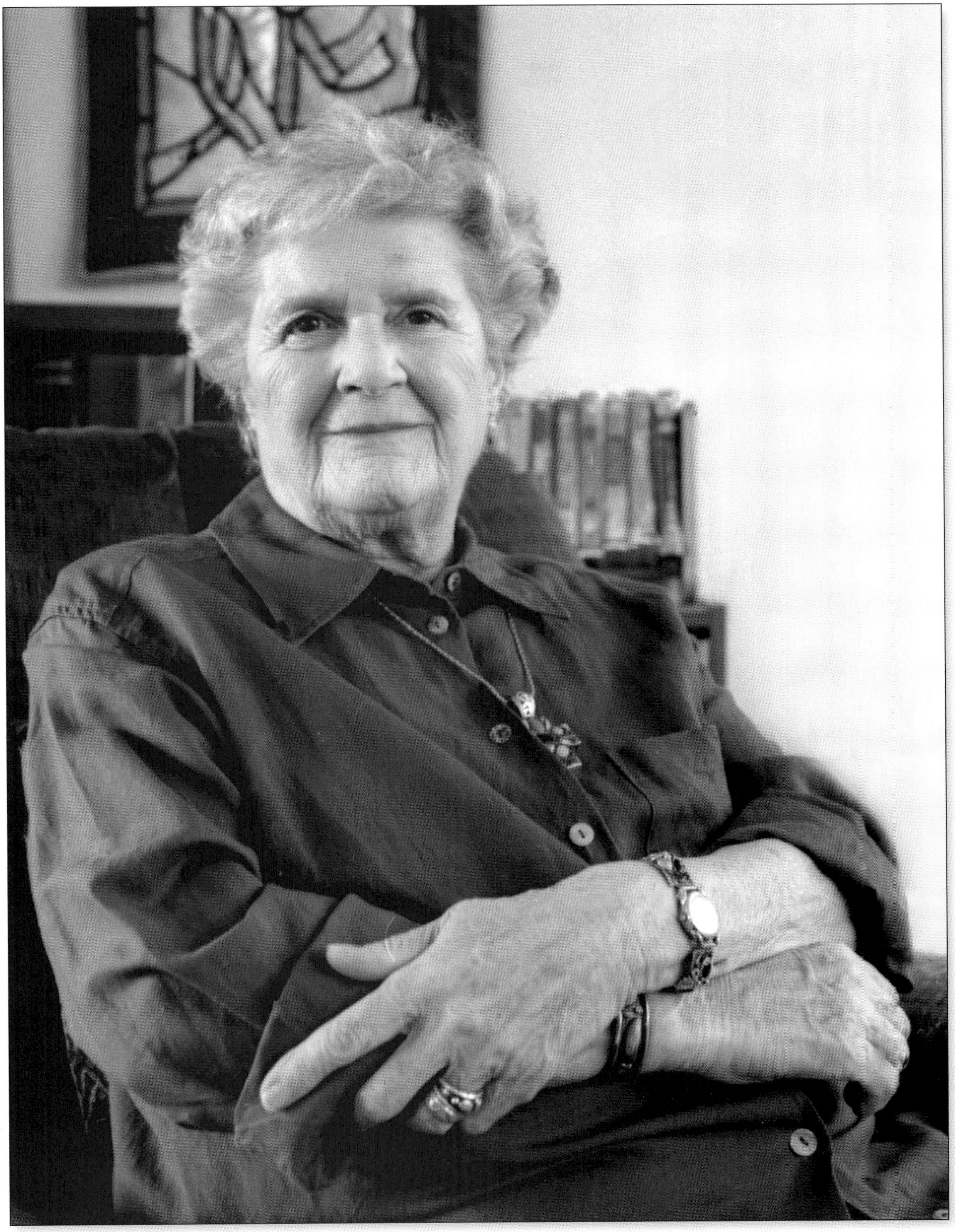

Marian (Smith) Moorman

- ✦ (WAC) U.S. Women's Army Corps, May, 1943–1945
- ✦ Civilian employee 1945–1954
- ✦ Transferred to Sandia Labs 1954–1982—Clerical work

It was July 15, 1945, and Marian Smith had a date to the Non-Commissioned Officers (NCO) Club dance with U.S. Army SED Fred Dellenbaugh. It was still early in the evening when the call came for Dellenbaugh and many of the other SEDs to go back to their barracks. Marian was not told the reason; this was Class A information, and she did not have Class A Security Clearance.

Dellenbaugh took Smith back to her dorm before heading to his barracks. The army men were told to get into their fatigues, bring their gear, and get into formation. It was all very strange and mysterious.

"It was a disappointment for me as I had been looking forward to having a good time at the dance; instead, I had an evening alone in my dorm, but I knew not to ask questions."

That was the night before the atomic bomb test at Trinity Site in the early morning of July 16, 1945. It was only afterwards that Moorman learned of the real reason. She didn't know it at the time, but she had inadvertently been caught up in the momentum preceding the first real test of the atomic bomb. What a historical night! ✦

Marian Cox, left, with Marian Smith

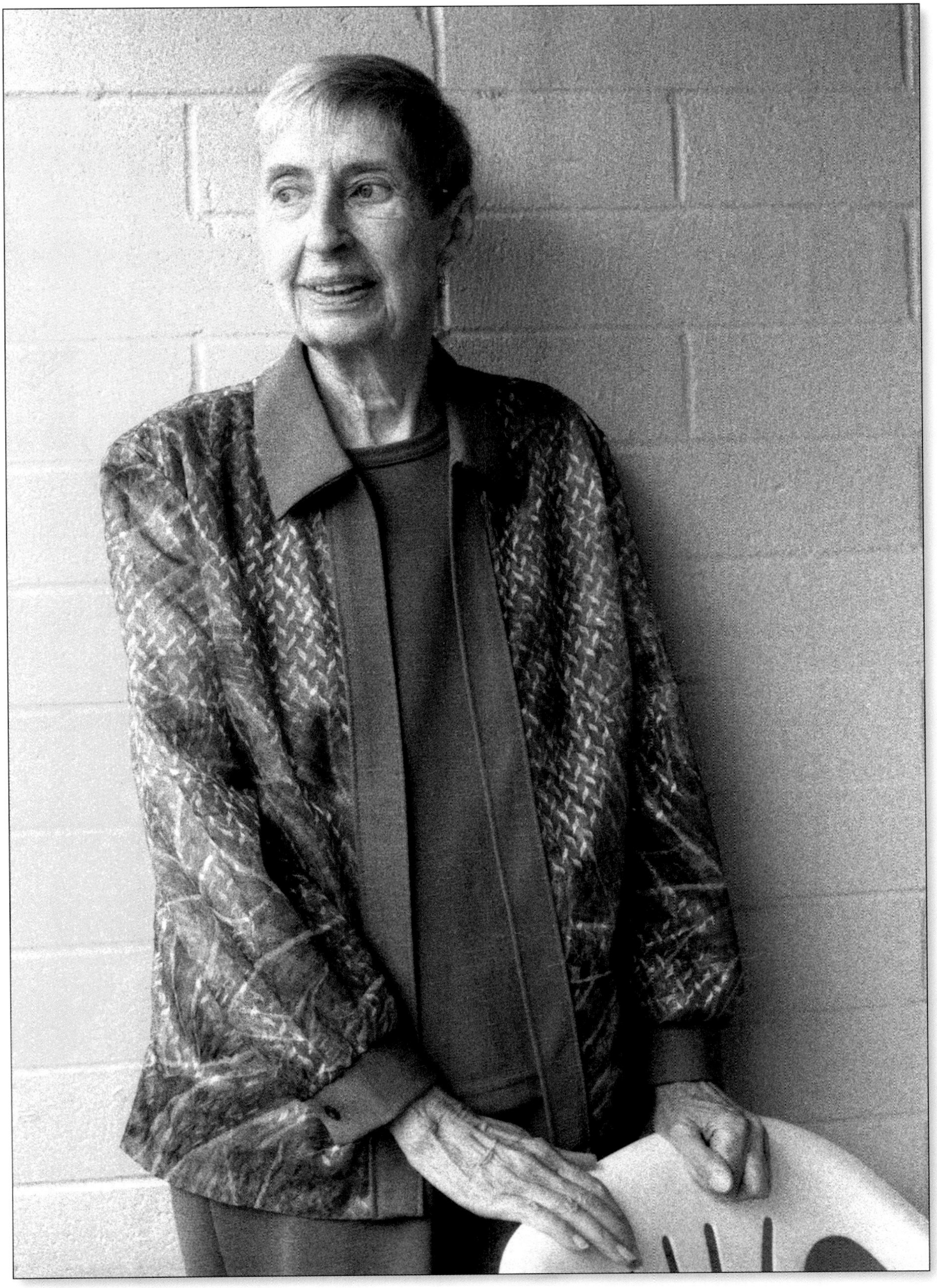

George Moulton, civilian

- Chemist, worked January, 1944–1977
- Worked eventually with polonium which was transferred into an initiator which went into the atomic bomb known as "Fat Boy"

George Moulton says he knew when the atomic bomb was to be tested at Trinity Site, but he was not to be part of the official spectators. That didn't slow him down too much.

He and three friends piled into his car and headed to Trinity Site that July day in 1945, unbeknownst to the officials there. Parking in a gully, dodging Military Police, and encountering an unfriendly red ant colony, the four finally reached a hill opposite to where the official observers were stationed. There they spent the night.

Searchlights bathed Trinity Site around 4:30 am. When nothing happened by 5:30, the four guys got ready to leave, assuming that the test was called off or that the bomb had not worked.

"Then," Moulton said, "we saw the blast and could feel the heat from the explosion. What a sight it was!

"It worked!" the guys exclaimed.

About development of the atomic bomb at Los Alamos and subsequent bombs dropped on Japan, George noted, "I thought it was necessary, and I have no regrets. It ended the war and that was good. ✦

George Moulton in dormitory room

Moulton, left, with Jack Crom

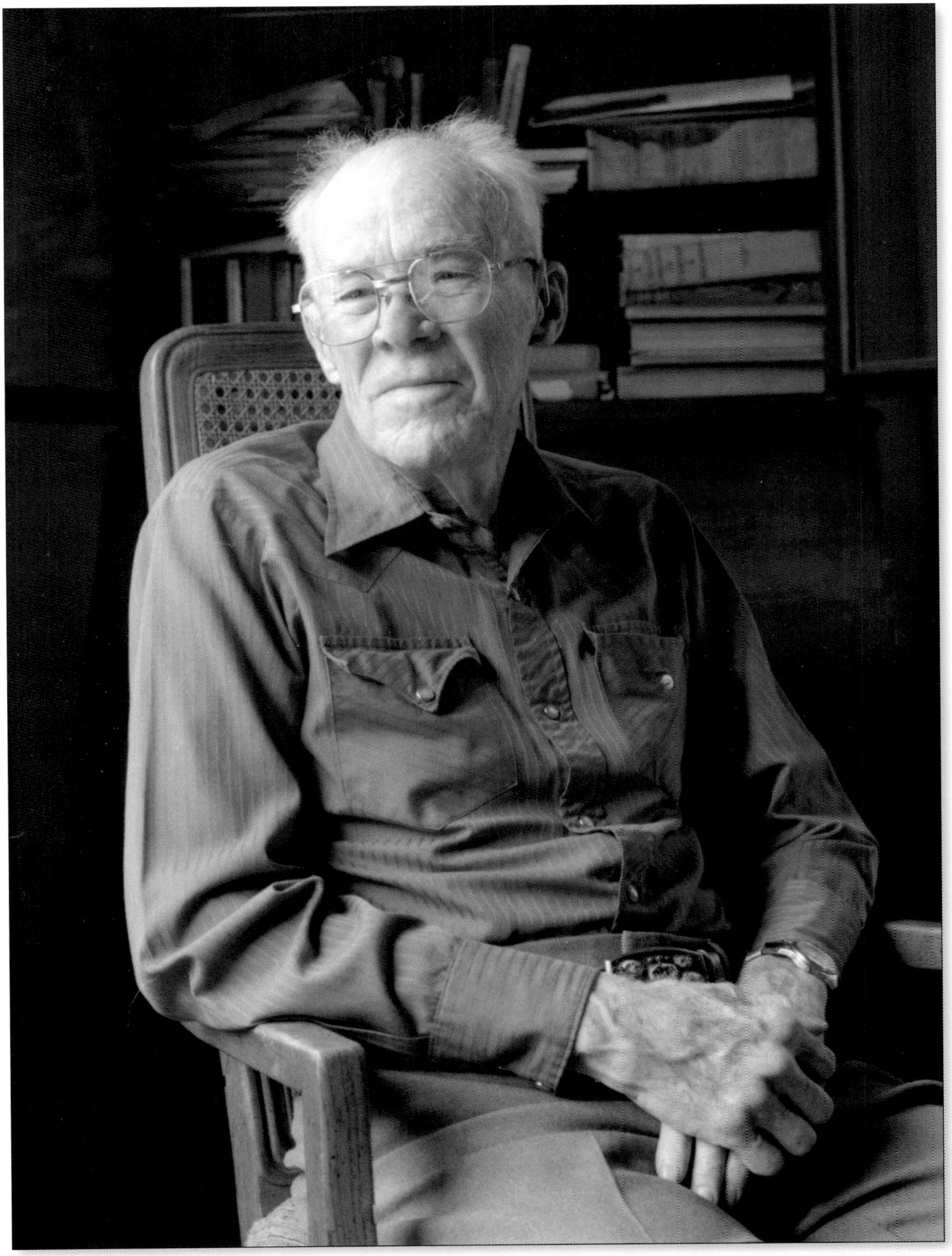

Jean (Parks) Nereson

- Sixth grade teacher, worked 1944-1995
- Central Elementary School

Jean Parks had a variety of positions before she was recruited to come to The Hill. She had been a teacher in Port Arthur, Texas, at an American school; at a Greek school, and then worked as a part-time saleslady. As she was working on her master's degree at the University of Minnesota, she first heard of the position at Los Alamos. She received letters from Dr. Walter W. Cook, the dean of education at the university, who was in Santa Fe for a speaking engagement. He wrote to her about a teaching position in New Mexico. He extolled the virtues of the position for a young woman. "He told me there were lots of parties and dances and eligible men, but he didn't say where the teaching position was located," Jean recalled.

She came to Los Alamos in the fall of 1944—where she lived in Dorm 237, a woman's dorm, and paid $15 a month for room and board.

"Dr. Cook had told me I was not going to a turquoise mine, and that I would be teaching well-cultured children. I had been hired to teach sixth grade, most of my students were the children of scientists. Their parents were definitely not the type of parents I had met before, and they were very involved in the school."

Dr. Cook had been hired to design the original school, and he specified a stage for each classroom. Parks made good use of that stage in her teaching. The students wrote the dialogue and directed Greek and Roman plays. (Parks was of Greek descent.) When a sewing machine became available from one of the wives who was leaving Los Alamos, Jean and four other teachers chipped in $5. each to buy it. With the sewing machine she was able to make a curtain for the stage as well as teach the children to sew costumes. (She kept the Singer sewing machine in her home.)

"I took the G.I. bus to Santa Fe every Saturday; I wanted to see the La Fonda Hotel as it was the only tall building in Santa Fe." There she bought material for the stage curtain and the costumes. (Parks paid for these herself).

Jean continued to communicate with two of her students of that year—Thelma Hagman of Santa Fe and Charlotte (Hagman) Duran of Rio Rancho. She made a lasting impression on most of her students.

In 1999, Jean (Parks) Nereson was selected as a "Living Treasure." This was the first year for the Los Alamos Living Treasure selections. ✦

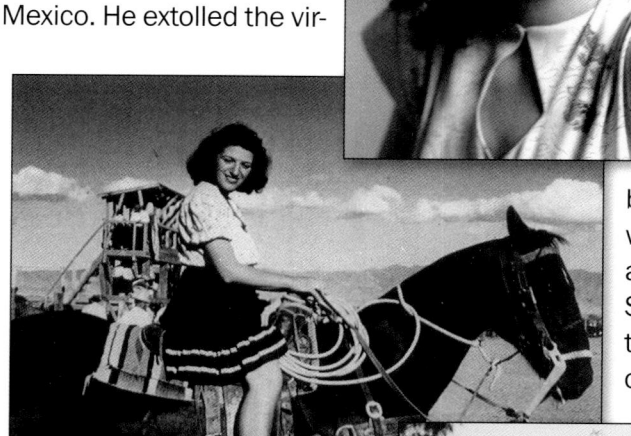

1944

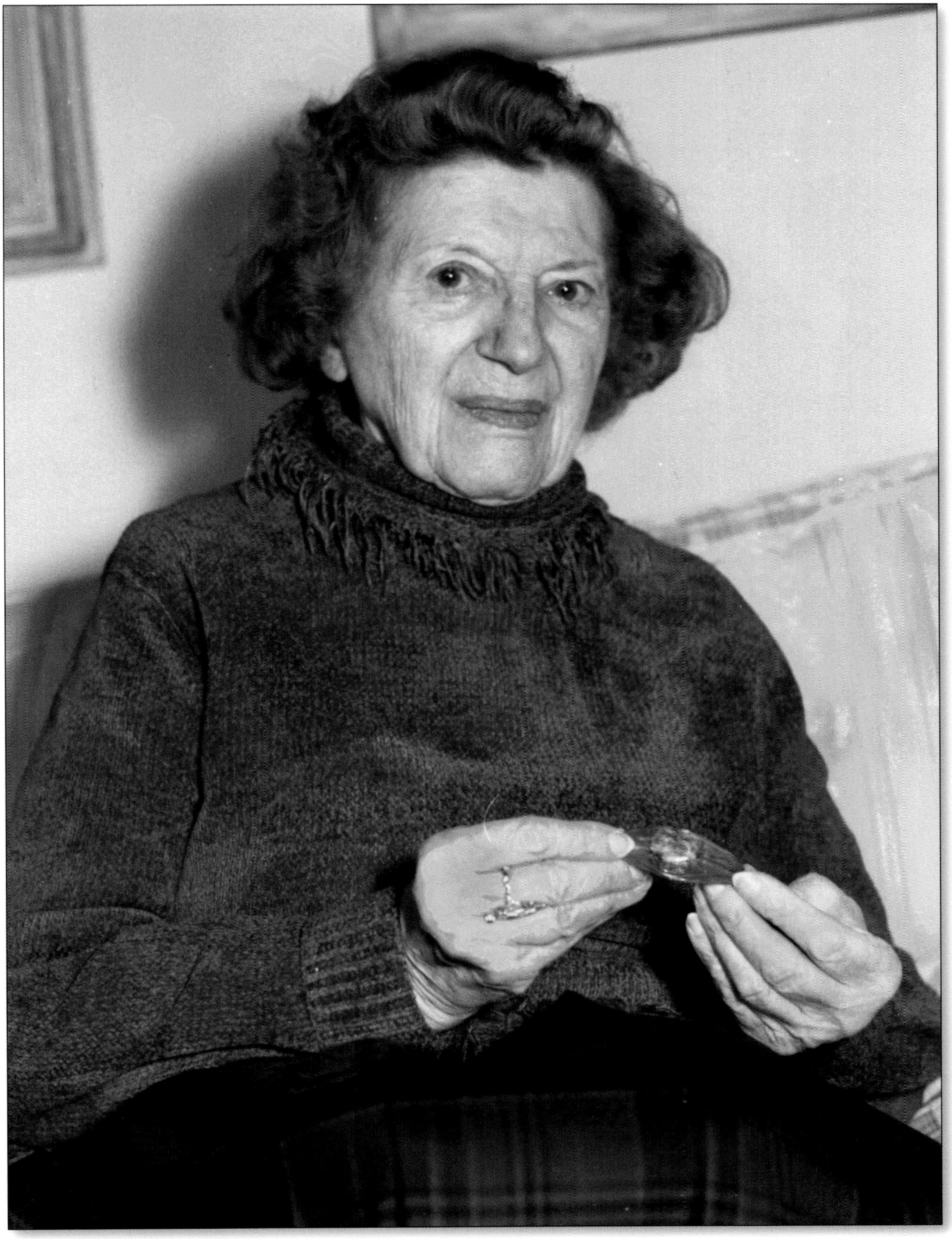

Willilam "Bill" Norwood, U.S. Army

- (SED) Special Engineer Detachment, March 12, 1945–1946
- Civilian employee 1946–1979
- Chemist, experience with explosives

In 1944, when the Battle of the Bulge was being fought in Europe, the U.S. needed more troops there. Bill Norwood was sent to Mississippi for ordnance training, six weeks of basic training, and three weeks of advance training. He fully expected to be sent overseas. So it was a shock to other military personnel as well as to Norwood himself when he was sent to Santa Fe, New Mexico. (People were frozen in their jobs and not usually transferred.) Norwood was asked if he had written his congressman to avoid being sent to Europe to which he answered, "No."

Norwood had numerous questions after he was deposited at the train station at Lamy. The first of his many questions was, "Why did the train not go to Santa Fe?" No answer. "How far is the base from Santa Fe?" he asked. "Two miles," was the answer. After checking in with Dorothy McKibbin at 109 E. Palace Ave. in Santa Fe, he was directed to the bus that would take him further. Other puzzling things were that McKibbin said she was expecting him, and no one in the office wore a uniform.

As the bus traveled the expected two miles and continued on, Norwood again asked a question of one of his bus companions: "How much longer is it before we are there?" He was told, "You'll find out, soldier." He asked a WAC, "How much farther is it?" and got the same answer, "You'll find out."

"Why don't you want to tell me?" he asked. No answer. "Where are we?" Answer: "You'll find out." The bus continued on its route through Pojoaque, finally stopping at the guard station at the entrance to The Hill. Because Norwood had no ID badge, he had to get off the bus. First Sergeant Winston Dabney was there with a car to take him to the barracks. Norwood still had no idea where he was.

Finally Norwood learned why no one would answer his numerous questions. It seems that army security personnel regularly rode the bus and asked similar questions. They were testing the bus riders to see if any information would be divulged.

About the Project, Norwood said: "Everyone in the nation was behind the war effort. People wanted Hitler and the Japanese out of countries where they didn't belong. "I finally received the answer to my last question, 'Why am I here?' It was my work at Los Alamos which helped hasten the end of the war."

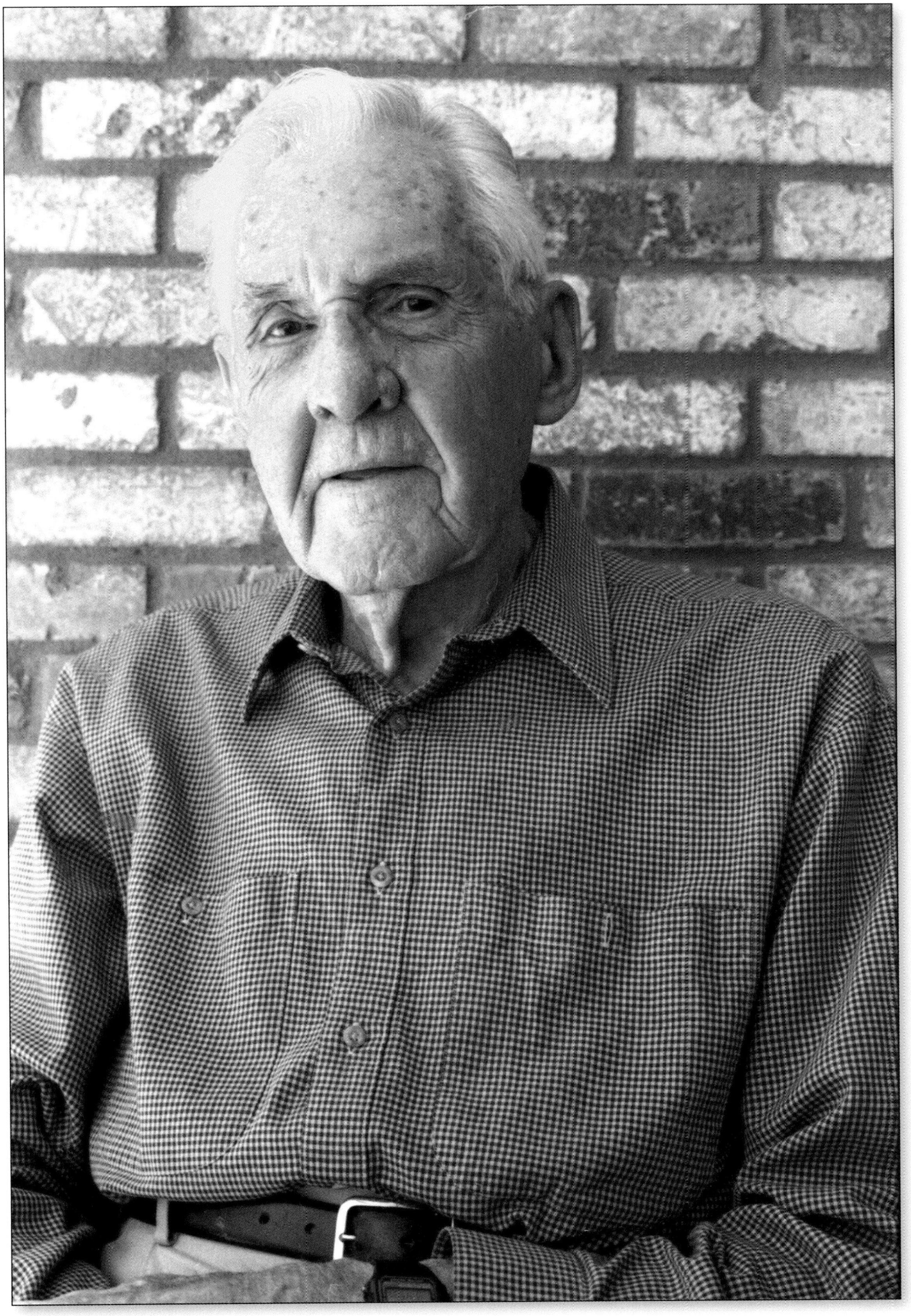

Florence (Mullins) Osvath

- ✦ Chemistry/Metallurgy Research Division, worked August 1, 1945–1951
- ✦ Kept records of radiation exposure and checked the amount of exposure on individuals

Florence Mullins was graduated from Mary Hardin-Baylor College in Belton, Texas (near Dallas) as a chemistry teacher. Not satisfied with just teaching, though Mullins wanted to use her chemistry education to help the war effort. She wrote to the War Board in Dallas, and received a letter offering her a position in the CMR Division at Los Alamos. She did not know at the time where the job was.

When she arrived on The Hill, she was put in the health instruments group, which kept records of radiation exposure. It was important to check the people who worked with radiation for any exposure.

"I found out that something was being done at the Lab to end the war within one month. My brother was in Europe and due to fly his fighter bomber to Japan. That is all I could think about at this time. Anything that would end the war before he flew his mission to Japan was a positive thing, I thought.

"Then, on August 6, 1945, the dropping of the first atomic bomb at Hiroshima was announced over the loudspeakers in the building. All of the scientists in the division came out into the hall so that they could better hear the proclamation. Many had tears in their eyes and mixed emotions about the "havoc that surely would have been wreaked."

On August 14, 1945, Japan surrendered to the Allies, marking the end of World War II. "I could feel good about my contribution to the war effort and the successful end of the war," Osvath concluded. ✦

103

Frank Osvath, civilian

- Machinist, worked August, 1943–1946, 1947–1983
- (Made one of Berlyn Brixner's high-speed cameras from a sketch photographer Brixner provided)

From Ford Motor Company, and then to a trade school, Frank Osvath was offered a position at "a place in New Mexico where he would be restricted to within a few miles and couldn't come back." Twenty-three-year-old Osvath would be deferred from the army, and he was told, he would not have to go to war if he transferred to The Hill. This was too good an offer to pass up, he thought. He went to work at Los Alamos.

Osvath knew about the upcoming test of the atomic bomb on July 16, 1945, at Trinity Site and decided he wanted to witness the event.

"Two days before the momentous day, six other fellows and I went to the area we had picked out. It was a long trek up a rough and treacherous trail to the top of North Baldy Peak to wait it out. Tired from our long climb, we all slept at the top of the mountain that night."

Early in the morning on that fateful and historic day, they got ready to watch the test from their high vantage point. They waited...and they waited...and they waited. The sun was beginning to appear over the horizon but nothing was happening. "I thought it was a dud," remembers Osvath.

"And then we felt the shock waves, even at our twelve-thousand-foot height, even at forty miles from the site of the blast. Only a few of us knew about the test. It was something to behold! It was something we would never forget!"

Osvath's deferment expired after the war, and he had to serve one year in the army in the Philippines. He waited for security clearance all summer of '47 in order to return to Los Alamos. In the interim he worked in a uranium machine shop. Altogether he spent forty years of his life working and living in Los Alamos.

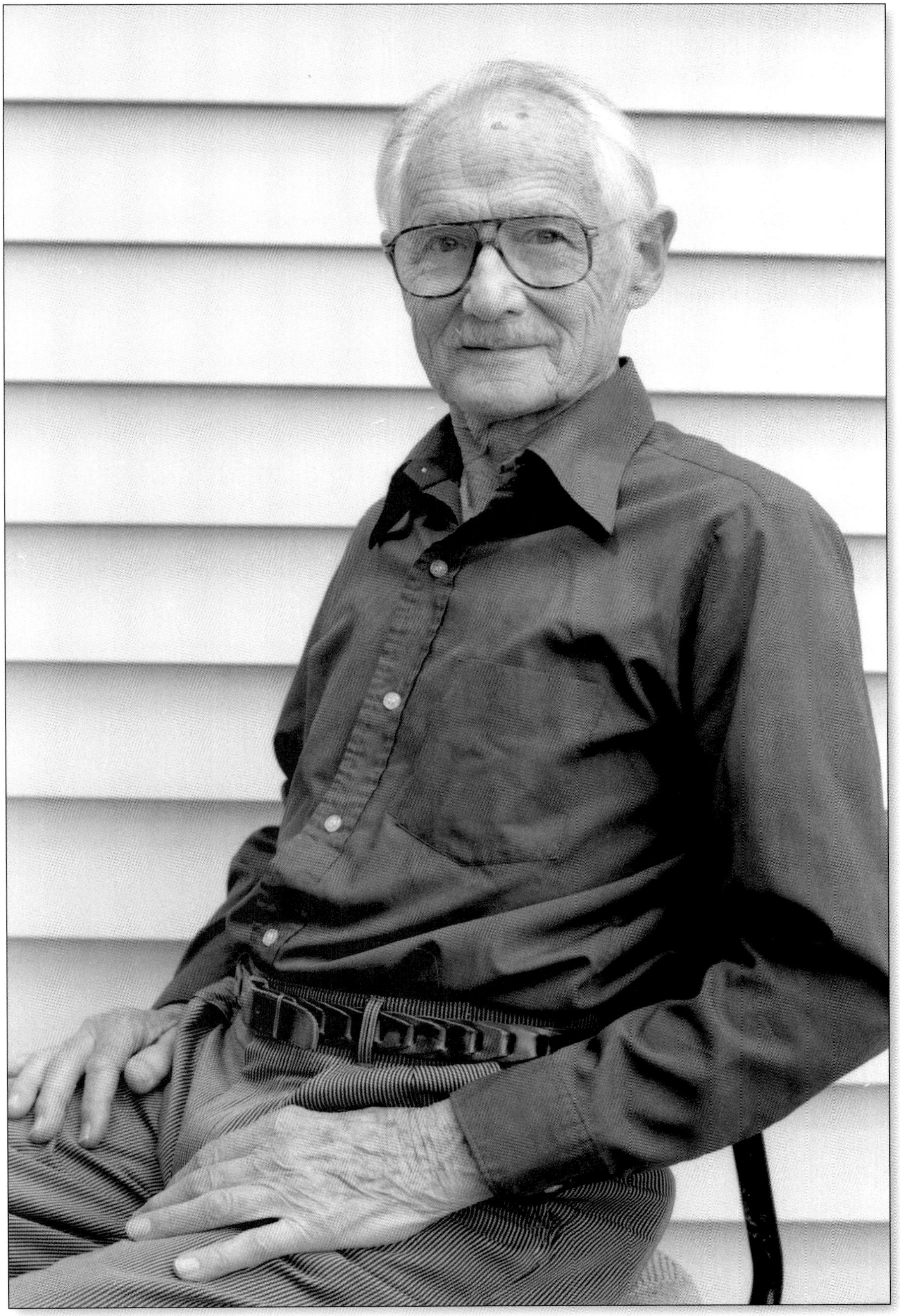

René J. Prestwood, civilian

- René J. Prestwood, civilian, worked April 22, 1943–1984
- Nuclear chemist
- Made the neutron source in the atomic bomb that was dropped on Nagasaki, Japan

---

René Prestwood arrived by train at Lamy, New Mexico, and took a bus to Santa Fe. It was there that he started looking for 109 E. Palace and Dorothy McKibbin. He noticed that wherever he went, so did the man behind him. Someone was following him. Was it a spy, he wondered? The authorities had warned him to be on the lookout for spies at this secret project.

He turned down one street, looking for his destination. So did the man behind him. So he changed streets and turned to lose the man behind him. He performed this strategy again and again, but the mysterious stranger stuck to him like glue.

At long last, he found the office he was looking for and stepped inside. So did the man behind him. It turned out that this man was headed for Los Alamos too. It was Nicholas Metropolis.

"Nick thought I was a spy too," laughed Prestwood. "I was relieved to find that he wasn't one." The two men ended up being temporary roommates at Cable's Ranch, which had cabana-type accommodations, until the first men's dorm, number T-102, was completed.

Preston remembers the weekly colloquium when all of the scientists gave updates on the progress in their particular areas, with Oppenheimer presiding. "Six outstanding scientists sat in the front row: Isidor Rabi, Enrico Fermi, Niels Bohr, Arthur Holley Compton, E. O. Lawrence, and Dick Feynman, all either science Nobel prize-winners or future recipients of that prestigious award."

"No one wore protective gear while working with dangerous materials," Prestwood remembered. "There never would have been a bomb if we had the same safety regulations in those days that are mandatory today."

"I don't regret working on the bomb. I would do it again for sure. I watched the test at Trinity Site from Sawyer's Hill. The whole sky lit up; then there was a low rumble, like distant thunder. Afterwards, the champagne flowed," he concluded. ✦

Nicholas Metropolis

Graduation at Berkley, 1942

At Los Alamos, 1943

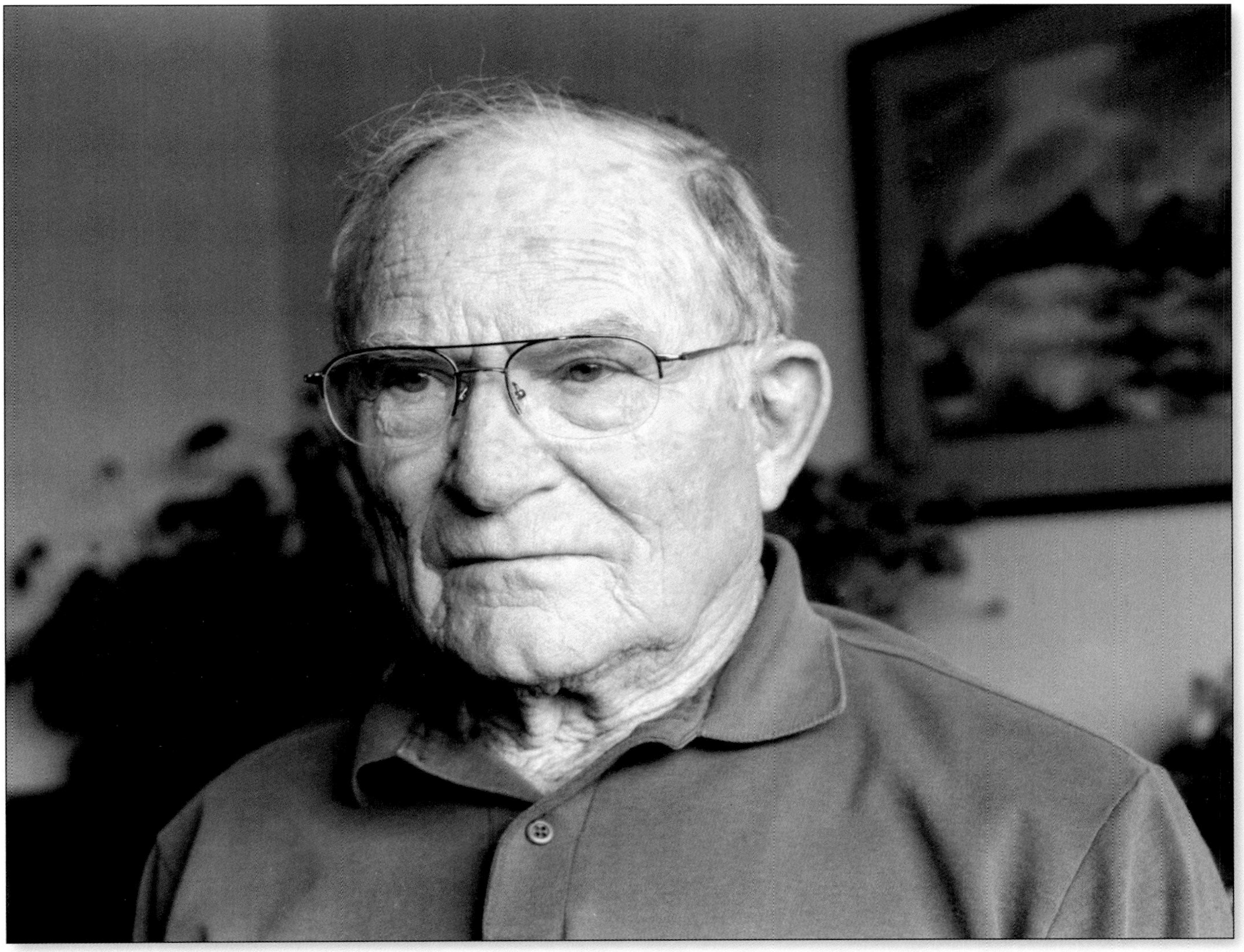

Jane (Keller) Rasmussen

- ✦ (WAC) U.S. Women's Army Corps, January, 1945–1946
- ✦ Telephone operator
- ✦ Civilian employee 1952–1990—Worked with computers

Jane Keller came to Los Alamos from Pennsylvania, exchanging her larger salary at Bell Telephone Company for the meager paycheck of a WAC, all for the war effort.

On The Hill she settled into doing what she knew: operating a switchboard, connecting phone lines by plugging them in. "There were only six pages of phone numbers," she emphasized.

"One day one of the bigwigs called me and wanted to be connected to a particular phone number. Unfortunately, he was asking to be connected to the same number he was on. I told him that politely, but he kept asking me to do the impossible. The third time he asked me, getting huffy about it, I yelled at him 'You are *on* that damn line!' I wanted to call him a dumb ass, but I restrained myself."

That was the day she almost got fired. When Keller was called "on the carpet,' she was frightened about what might happen. "My boss Nellie Rushing called me in and chewed me out for being rude. 'You should have given him the number he wanted anyway,' she said."

Another incident Rasmussen remembered was leaving the grounds to go to Santa Fe. Of course, she had to go through security check at the guard station and show her ID badge. "I don't know why I did it, but I handed the guard a one dollar bill. Years later as I again passed through that particular guard station, the MP remembered me and said, 'Hi, Jane,' handing me a one collar bill." ✦

Jane and Roger Rasmussen's wedding

Nellie Rushing
(Courtesy of Los Alamos National Lab Archives)

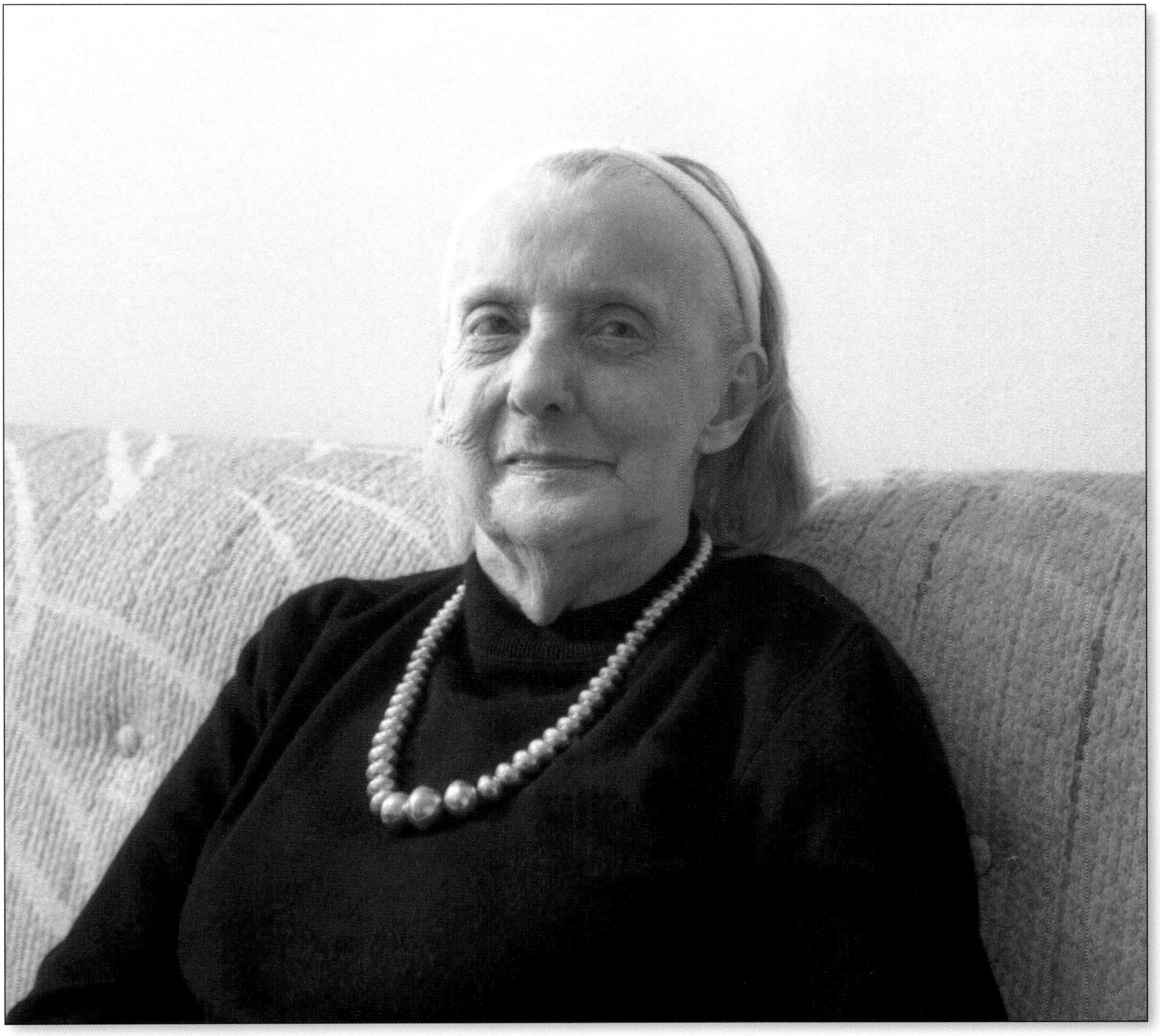

Roger Rasmussen, U.S. Army

- ✦ (SED) Special Engineer Detachment, January, 1945–1946
- ✦ Civilian employee 1946–1982
- ✦ Physicist—Built electronics for after-test diagnostics at Trinity Site

---

Roger Rasmussen was drafted into the army in June, 1943. The Army Specialized Training Program tested him and sent him for advanced training. He pursued scientific studies at the University of West Virginia and also at Lafayette College in Pennsylvania. Then he was transferred to The Hill for work in the Lab on development of the atomic bomb.

It was business as usual when fires broke out in the summer at Los Alamos. The SEDs, Rasmussen among them, were each given a shovel, loaded into a bus and driven to Santa Clara Canyon to fight the fire.

"I was a city boy and didn't know about fighting fires," recalled Rasmussen. "I didn't know what to do with the shovel, and I couldn't even find the fire." Ramussen wandered around in the forest for hours and managed to get lost. "I found the base camp only after the bus had left," he reported. "Finally, the next morning, I was missed, and someone came back and picked me up. It was not a pleasant experience."

Roger Rasmussen met Jane Keller shortly after they both arrived in Los Alamos. A courtship soon began. Roger really liked being invited to the WAC's mess hall for Sunday lunch. The food was better and it was clean there. In contrast, he spoke about the army mess: "Often the lights would go out while we were eating. Everyone would stop eating until the lights went back on. This was because there were cockroaches and you didn't want to mistake the cockroach for the food on your plate. Actually, the roaches would make off with your meal."

One of eight in his team at Trinity Site on July 16, 1945, Rasmussen lay under a truck when the first atomic bomb was detonated. "It was the brightest light I ever saw, even with my eyes closed," he asserted.

Roger Rasmussen and Jane Keller were married in November, 1945 at St. Francis Cathedral in Santa Fe. They had a son and a daughter and were married for more than sixty years. ✦

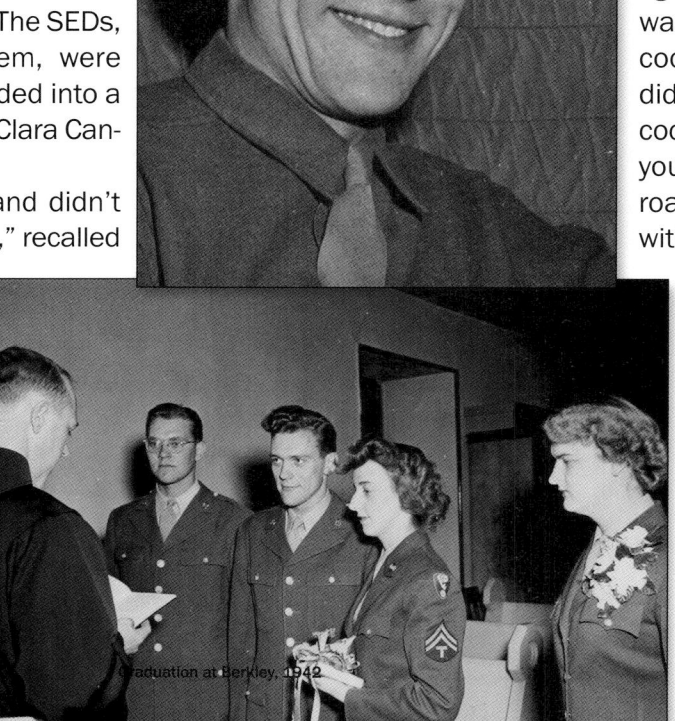

Graduation at Berkley, 1942

Rasmussen wedding, Mike Michnovicz, best man

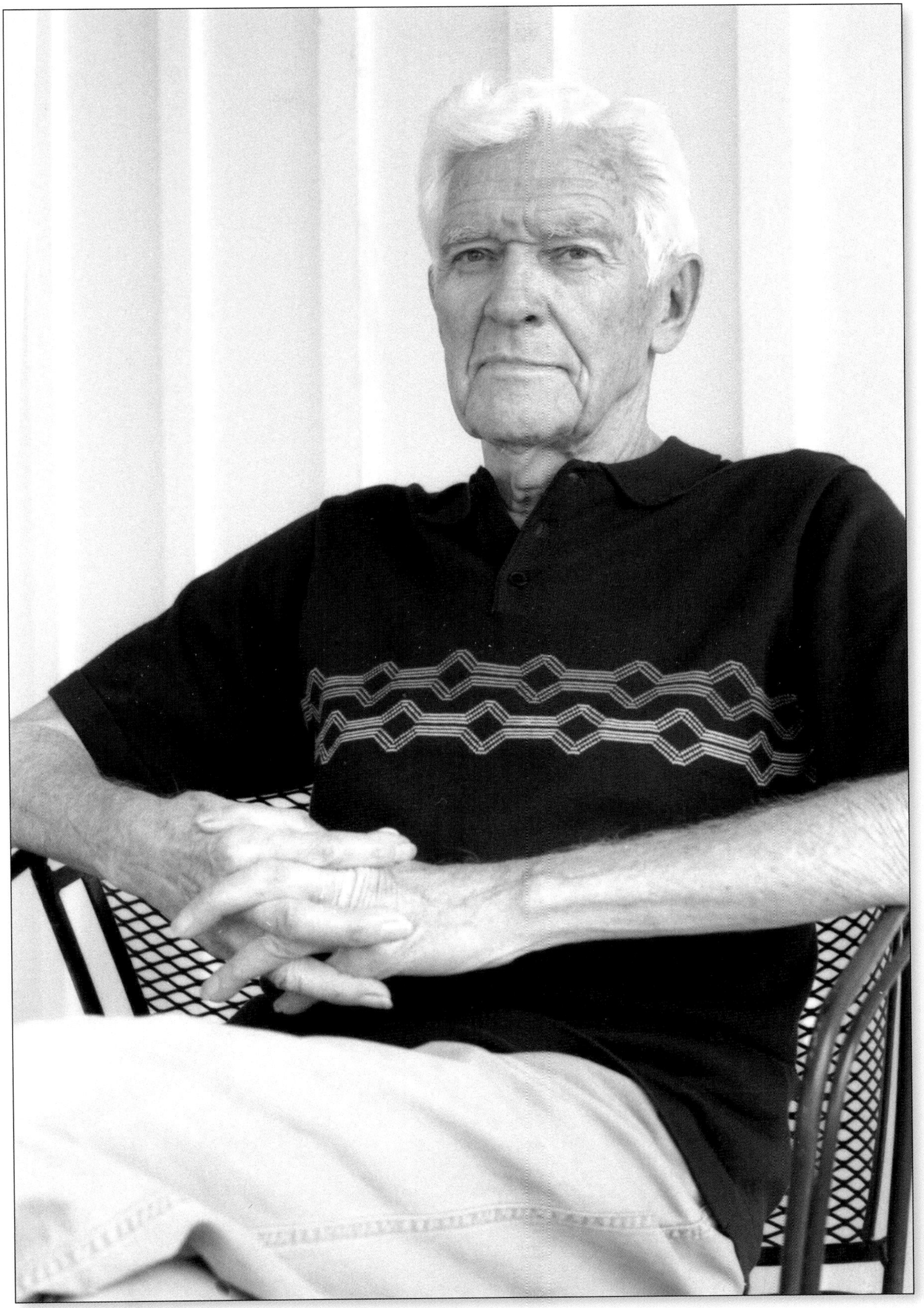

Louis Rosen, civilian

- Physicist, worked April, 1944–1990
- Worked with implosion technology

Louis Rosen remembers transporting explosives to the firing sites from the shack where the explosives were stored. On one occasion he rode with SED Mike Clancy to the site where the explosives were needed. Clancy drove the jeep while Rosen held fifty pounds of explosives on his lap. "There were no real roads in those days, and we were bounced and jounced along. I never thought about the danger of those explosives having such a rough ride. It could have been a disaster, but I came through it unscathed and unaware of the implications of our thoughtless actions."

Rosen tells of the antics of the practical joker, Dick Feynman, a brilliant scientist and former student of Hans Bethe. "He may have been the most brilliant of all of the scientists," Rosen declared, "and he liked to play tricks on people, especially the security personnel." On one occasion he replaced his ID badge photograph with a photo of a dog. That went unnoticed by security for weeks and weeks.

Feynman was adept at unlocking locks and three-way code numbers on safes. Often working at the Lab at night, Feynman would enter the office of someone who was not working. (He resented the fact that the scientist was *not* working.) He would then unlock the safe and leave it open. Security would discover the open safe—where classified documents were held—and issue a citation to the hapless victim.

While Feynman was on The Hill, his wife was in a hospital in Albuquerque suffering from tuberculosis. He wanted to be able to give his wife something to do while she was recuperating, so he would write her letters and cut them up before sending them. This drove the censors out of their minds. Finally General Groves had to intercede for him. The censors finally let it go. Other times he would write in Hebrew and other foreign languages.

"Feynman could not be fired because he was so brilliant. It would have set the development of the bomb back months and months. We could not afford that," ended Rosen.

Rosen has had more than a hundred articles published in professional journals on subjects including the fission process and the fusion process. He received the E.O. Lawrence Award for development of technology to detect and measure the energy of neutrons and charged nuclei. At the award ceremony he was presented a gold medal and a certificate signed by President John F. Kennedy.

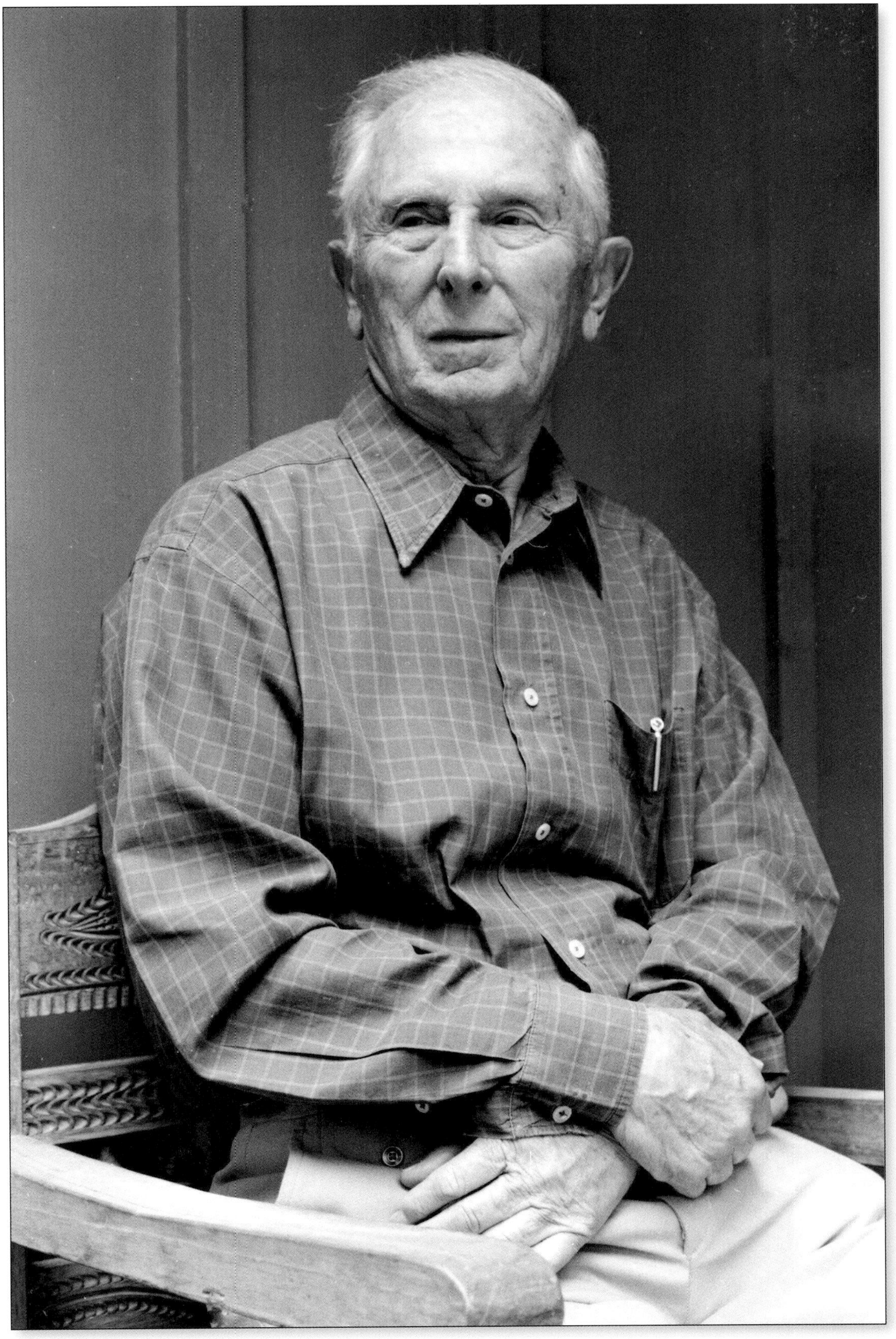

Julia (Dasheno) Roybal

+ Housekeeping and child care, worked 1944–1948
+ San Ildefonso Pueblo

Just before the Christmas holiday, 1944, the principal at St. Catherine's Indian School in Santa Fe, where Julia Dasheno attended high school, asked the girls if anyone wanted to work on The Hill during the break. Three girls responded to the offer and were transported to their destination by army truck. There they were fingerprinted and given ID badges that served as passes through the guarded gates.

"I earned $1.50 in the morning and $1.50 for the afternoon. I ironed shirts," reported Roybal. "When I babysat, I earned $2.50 for all day." During the summer of 1945, she worked in the Oppenheimer's home several times. She recalled that security men guarded outside the home.

After work, Dasheno enjoyed going to the PX with the other girls to get a Coke and sometimes ice cream. She was just sixteen years old that summer.

The young girls cleaned only the day room and hallways at the barracks, never the rooms of the occupants. One of the men made quite an impression on her. "We used to call him 'That bushy-headed man.' He wore tennis shoes with no shoe strings. I thought he was Albert Einstein, but I later found out that Einstein never visited The Hill. He was always nice and friendly and said good morning to us"

Dasheno had been traveling to Los Alamos with a friend (who later became her sister-in-law.) When the friend quit her job, so did Julia. "I didn't want to be there by myself," she said. But later she went back to cleaning houses on The Hill. "I liked going to the movies at Los Alamos; it cost just ten cents, and I liked to stay there for the weekend."

"Once I saw a poster with a picture of a big cloud on a bathroom door in one of the homes. At the time I didn't know what it was. Of course, later I found out that it was a photograph of the first test of the bomb down at Trinity Site," she ended. ✦

First bomb test at Trinity Site
(Photo, Jack Aeby. Courtesy of Los Alamos National Lab Archives)

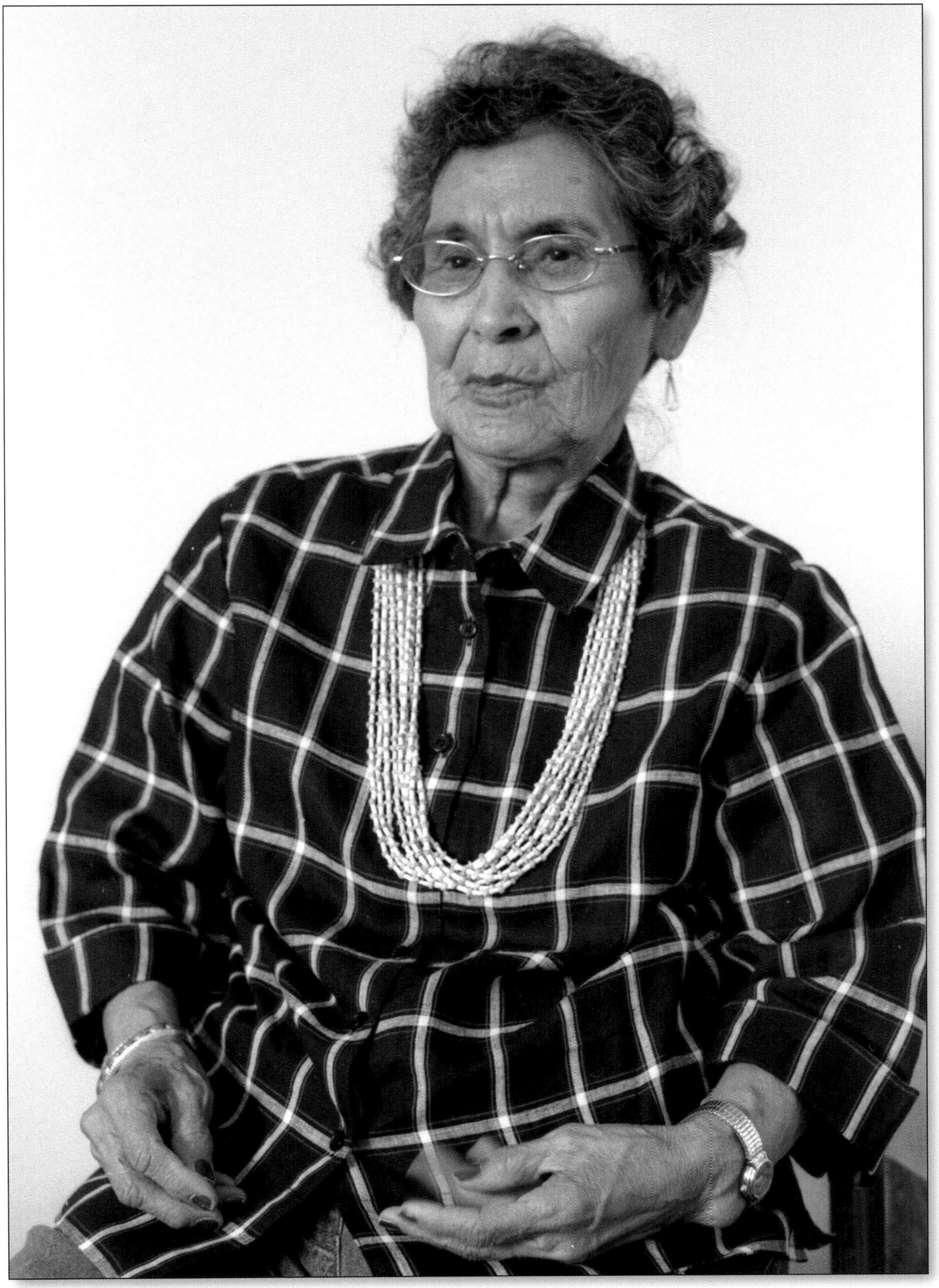

Ramon Sanchez

- ✦ Worked September, 1944-1945
- ✦ Worked as jack hammer operator, bus driver, truck driver

Ramon Sanchez had several jobs at Los Alamos. At first he used a jackhammer to loosen the frozen ground for preparing building foundations. After he received security clearance, he drove a delivery truck to the sites where experiments on the bomb were being conducted. Sometimes he drove Bus Number Thirteen to take people into Santa Fe for shopping expeditions, where they could buy items not available in Los Alamos.

"I did what I had to do and didn't ask any questions, he emphasized.

He tells of the experience that made a deep and lasting impression and ended his career at Los Alamos. One day he loaded his truck with steel shelves for a garage that was being assembled at one of the sites. His best buddy, Rafael Aguilar, was also driving a truckload of shelving to the site. Sanchez started out first, with his friend following. After a few minutes, he noticed that the second truck was no longer behind him. He waited a few minutes, but the second truck did not appear. Later he found out there had been a terrible accident. Aguilar had lost control of the loaded truck, and it rolled down the hill and landed right on top of him. Aguilar was killed.

Sanchez said he was subjected to many hours of interrogation. Officials wanted to know if the other driver had been drunk. Sanchez insisted he personally knew nothing about this, but they did not believe him. This really upset Sanchez, and he was fired, he says, because he refused to say Aguilar was drunk.

Sanchez later added that he thought the sun may have been in Aguilar's eyes and that caused him to run off the road. ✦

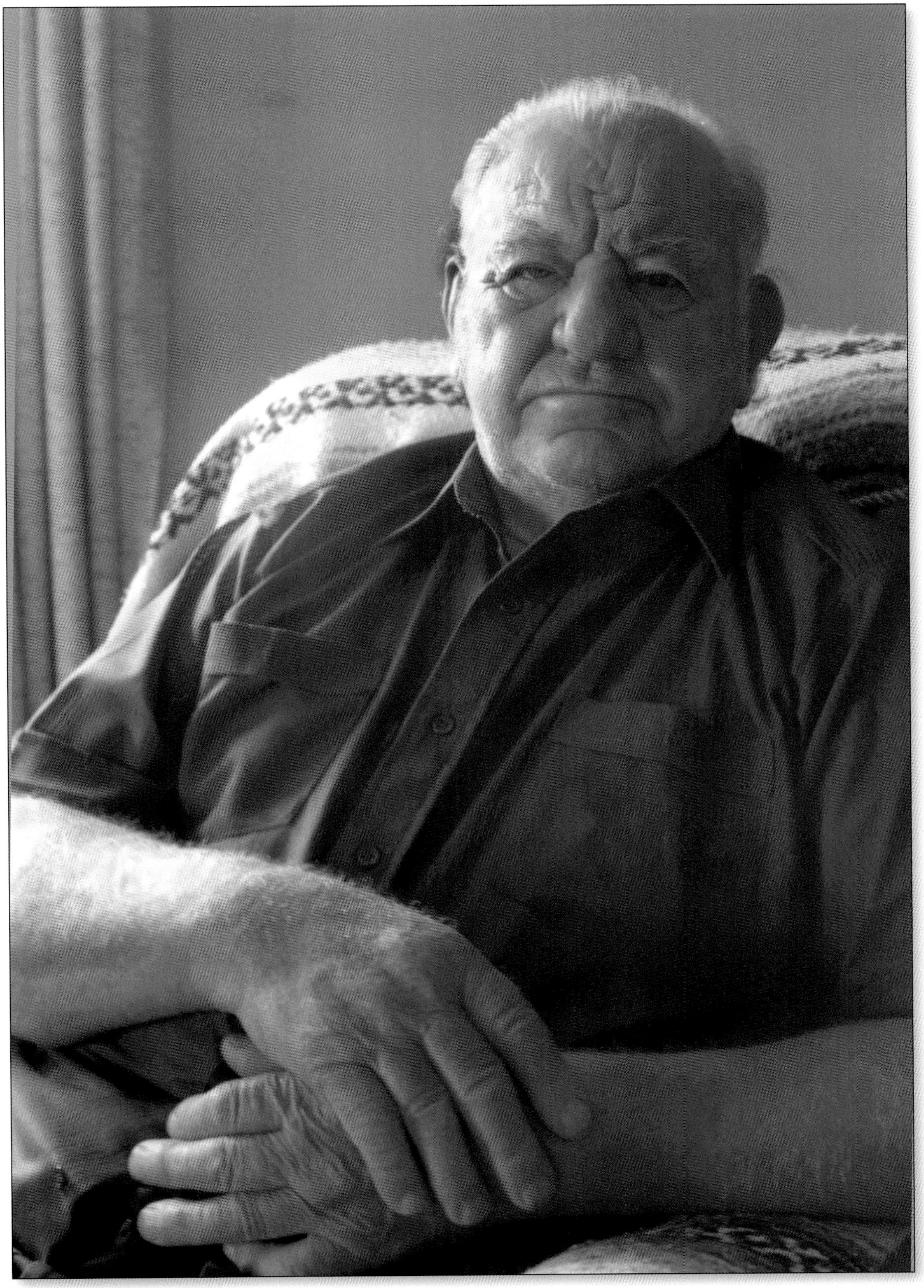

Secundo "Sec" Sandoval

- ✦ Elementary student during World War II
- ✦ Later mechanical designer and draftsman at Lab
- ✦ Became an artist

Jean Parks, an elementary teacher, told of Sec Sandoval's artistic beginnings while he was in the seventh grade. Parks taught the sixth grade but was friendly with Hilda Johnson, the seventh grade teacher whose classroom was across the hall. Parks had Clara Sandoval, Sec Sandoval's sister, in her class. The two teachers, who had playground supervision together, talked about Sandoval's artistic ability.

One day, Johnson showed Parks one of Sandoval's watercolors of Black Mesa, a sacred landmark to the people of San Ildefonso and Santa Clara pueblos. "It looked like a photograph," Nereson remembered.

On one of her trips to New York City, Parks took Sandoval's painting of Black Mesa as well as others by Los Alamos elementary students to the Metropolitan Museum of Art. The Met displayed all of the pictures in their gallery, but Sandoval's painting received the place of honor. He also received an award for it.

At the time, Parks purchased a book on *How to Draw* for Sandoval. "Sec said that book inspired him to become an artist," she reported.

"I always wanted to become an artist," Sandoval said, "ever since I got Donald Duck and Mickey Mouse coloring books." At first Sandoval worked in oils, but eventually he became allergic to the oils and had to switch to watercolors.

Sec Sandoval remembered the fireworks at Los Alamos celebrating the end of World War II. "There were fireworks all over the place. I wondered where they got them. I was just a kid at the

Sec Sandoval at an early age

time. I spent a lot of time back then picking up Coke bottles that the G.I.s had discarded so that I could get the deposit money."

He retired from the Lab at the age of thirty-nine after working there for fifteen years. ✦

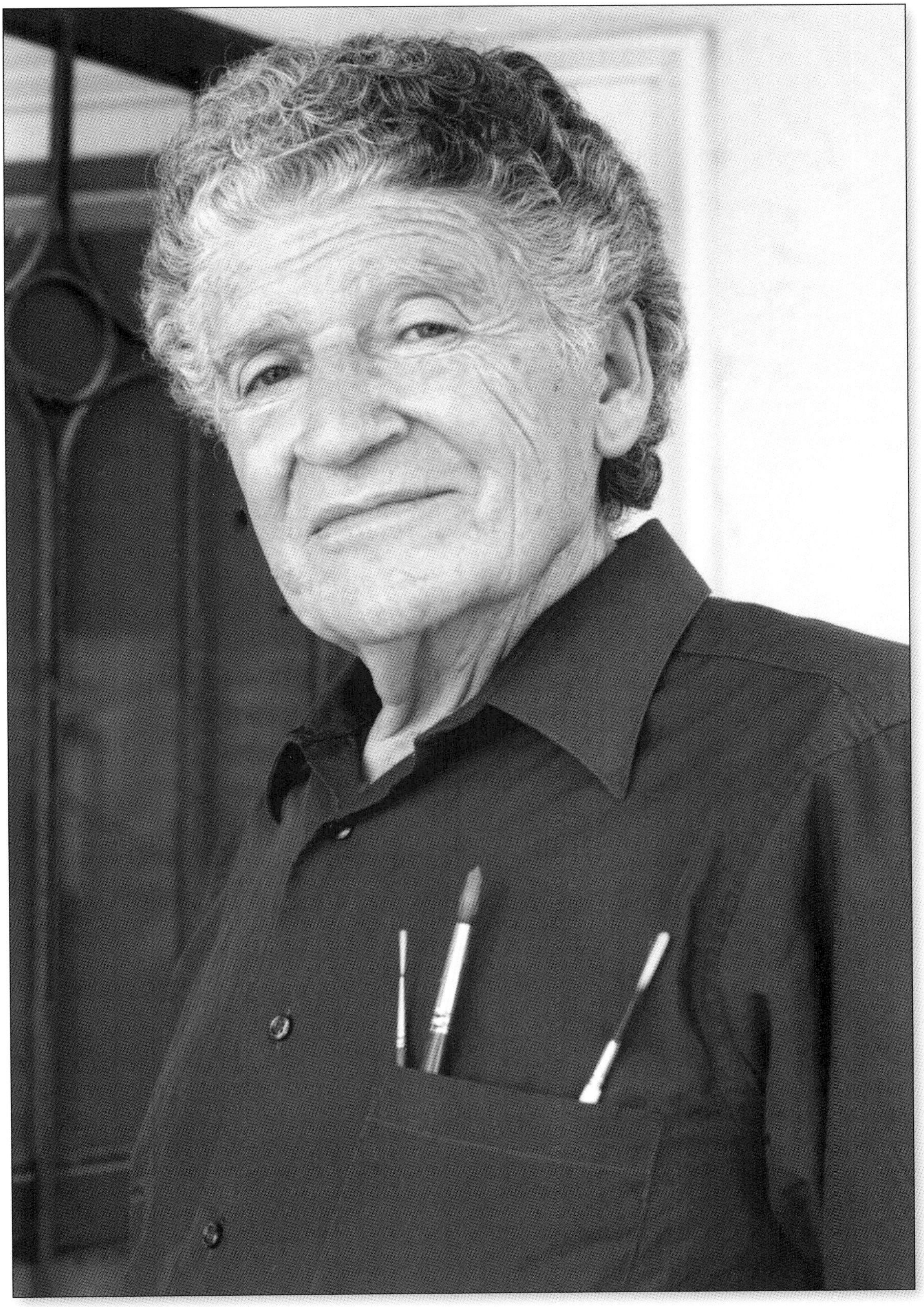

Arthur "Art" Schelberg, civilian

✦ Physicist, worked April, 1943–1982
✦ Worked on diagnostics for weapons

Contributing his part to a critical project, Art Schelberg found his work on the atomic bomb interesting and challenging.

"One of the most important components to building the bomb was the method of triggering it. It was necessary to instantaneously and uniformly compress the uranium into a ball of critical mass. To test our idea, we built a one-third scale model of the proposed final device—a sphere with thirty-two electrically-fired explosive detonators (which we called "guns") spaced uniformly around it," Schellberg stated.

The high-voltage electricity for firing the detonators was provided by capacitors charged by a generator. The generator was powered from a set of batteries which were enclosed in metal containers. The batteries were connected in-parallel for charging; then, to provide a higher voltage for the generator, the battery connections were switched to series. During charging the batteries gave off combustible gas as an automobile battery does.

One day, as the batteries were being switched from parallel to series, an explosion blew the cover off one of the battery boxes. There must have been a loose connection which produced a spark and ignited the combustible gas. As you can imagine, the explosion was unexpected and gave us quite a jolt, noted Schelberg.

"I am glad that the bomb worked. About the destruction of Hiroshima, well, that's just a part of war. Any action that shortens war is desirable."

When Art's brother-in-law returned from the service, he told Art, "Thank you. You saved me from having to go to a Pacific battle front. I know I would most likely have been killed."

Invasion of Japan had been scheduled by the War Department for November, 1945. Fortunately, it was not necessary. World War II ended with the surrender of Japan after the atomic bombs were dropped in early August. It is estimated that more than half a million U.S. troops surely would have been killed if the invasion of Japan had been necessary. ✦

(Courtesy of Los Alamos National Lab Archives)

1943 near Taos: Ben Diven, left, Art Schelberg driving, and Ernie Klema, right

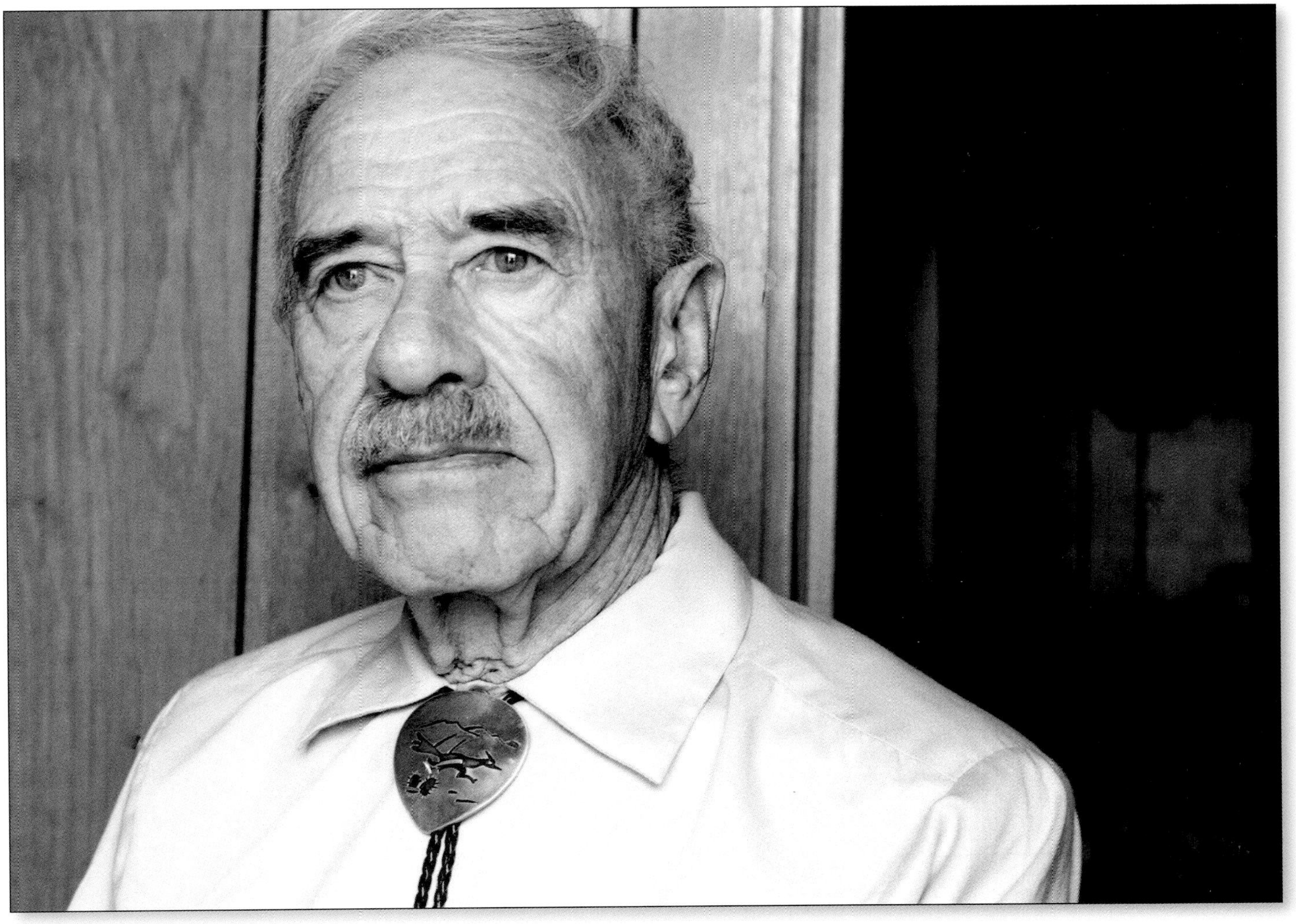

Marguerite "Marge' Schreiber

✦ Wife of Scientist Raemer "Schreib" Schreiber
✦ Lived on The Hill November, 1943–February, 1999

Marge Schreiber told how she, her husband, Raemer, and baby daughter, Paula Christine, came to live in Los Alamos. The war was on and it was summer. The Schreibers had been living at that time in Lafayette, Indiana. Schreib came home for lunch one day and he said to her "What would you think about going to Santa Fe this fall?"

Schreiber continued, "Schreib had finished his doctorate in physics the year before, in June, 1942 at Purdue University. There was nothing that would keep us from saying okay and so we went. However, Raemer could not tell me what he would do there, and I couldn't tell anyone where we were going."

One occurrence at Los Alamos was indelibly imprinted on Marge's memory. It was a quiet afternoon in early August, 1945, before the atomic bomb was dropped on Hiroshima, about 3 pm. The two little girls, Paula and Sara, were napping in the bedroom.

"Schreib came in, which was unusual at that time of day, and he had a bundle of his clothing with him. He said there had been an accident at the Lab; Louis Sloten was doing a demonstration and his tool had slipped, causing him to be exposed to radiation. Another man was close and probably had received some radiation also. Schreib, too, was in the Lab at the time, but he thought he and a few others were far enough away to not be exposed. Then Schreib went to the hospital for observation for three days.

"Harriet Hollaway was at the foot of my porch stairs and, after I told her, we just looked at each other. In times of crisis, we would take out the whiskey bottle, so Harriet went and got her bottle. Every time I looked like I was going to faint, Harriet would give me another shot of whiskey. I have no idea how much I drank during that time, but I am certain I completely depleted her supply. Consequently, I have no real memory of that night, and that's how I got through it."

A neighbor took the children, fed them, and put them to sleep, telling them that Mommy was busy. All of the Schreibers' friends came to lend support too.

The hospital observation proved Raemer had not been exposed to radiation. Marge said she went to the hospital daily but was not allowed see Louie, who later died.

"Louie and Schreib were to load the bomb, and Schreib told me he didn't *have* to go, but I said he did, and so he went. I was proud of the men who worked on the atomic bomb. They did what they had to do to win the war." ✦

Marge and Raemer Schreiber and Kachina
(Courtesy of Los Alamos National Lab Archives)

Louis Sloten
(Courtesy of Los Alamos National Lab Archives)

122

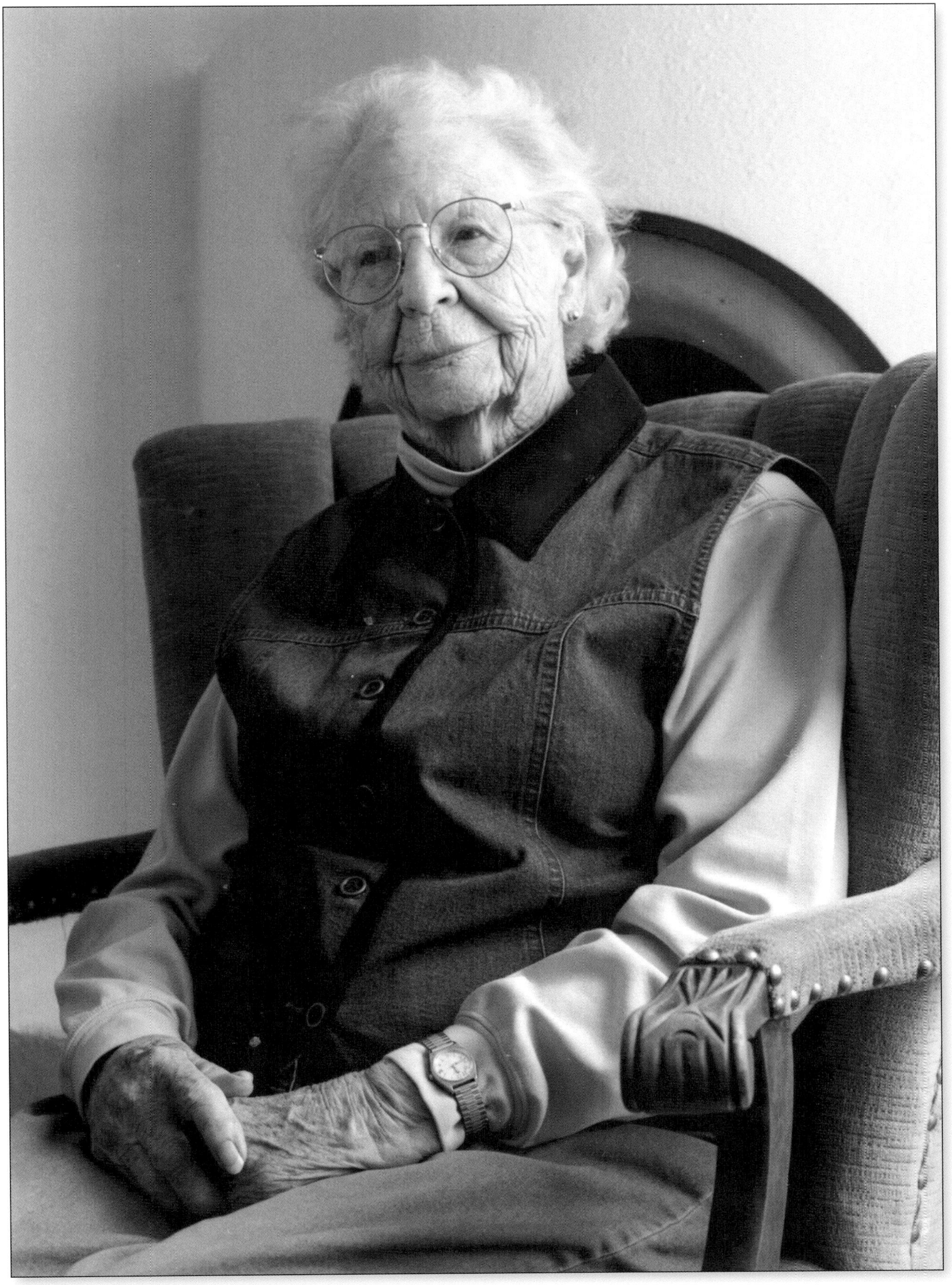

Haskell Sheinberg, U.S. Army

- ✦ (SED) Special Engineer Detachment, 1944–1946
- ✦ Civilian employee 1946–1990
- ✦ Chemical engineer
- ✦ Plutonium group, later powder metallurgy, and ceramics

It all happened in 1945, while the war was still in progress. Haskell Sheinberg was recovering from a hernia operation; sharing his hospital room was a man with a broken leg. (For the sake of identification, let's call this man Lloyd Johnson, as his real name cannot be recalled.)

One day, who should come to visit but Sheinberg's girl friend, WAC Beatrice Freeman. The two chatted for a few minutes. Then, from the next bed came the pitiful bleat of Johnson.

"Oh, I am so thirsty," complained Johnson. "I haven't had a beer in two days."

He beseeched Freeman to go to the PX and get him some beer. Feeling sorry for Johnson, Freeman left the hospital and went to the PX for the beer. In a few minutes she returned with a couple of bottles of beer.

Only 3.2% beer was allowed on The Hill at that time. Johnson eagerly opened the first of the two bottles, and, surprise: the beer went *splaaat*. It sprayed the ceiling, it sprayed the walls, it sprayed the bed sheets, it sprayed the people in the room.

"Oh, well," said Johnson, "I'll open the next one more slowly and carefully." He took the opener and meticulously removed the cap from the bottle. Same song, second verse: the beer showered everyone and everything in the room again."It smelled just like a brewery," Sheinberg recalled. Sheinberg, Freeman, and Johnson were convulsed in laughter.

In the midst of all of this merriment, in walks Ernestine, the nurse, who was also a lieutenant in the WACs and outranked the others in the room.

(Courtesy of Los Alamos National Lab Archives)

She was a tall woman, about five foot eight, and capable of infinite anger. She let out a bellow. "I am going to call Clarence Berg (administrator of the hospital) and he will take care of you properly!" With that edict she turned abruptly and stomped out of the room.

That put a damper on the festive atmosphere in the room, but everyone survived the incident. Sheinberg laughed long and hard about that "green" beer which had probably been brewed in too much of a hurry because of the war.

And Berg never came… ✦

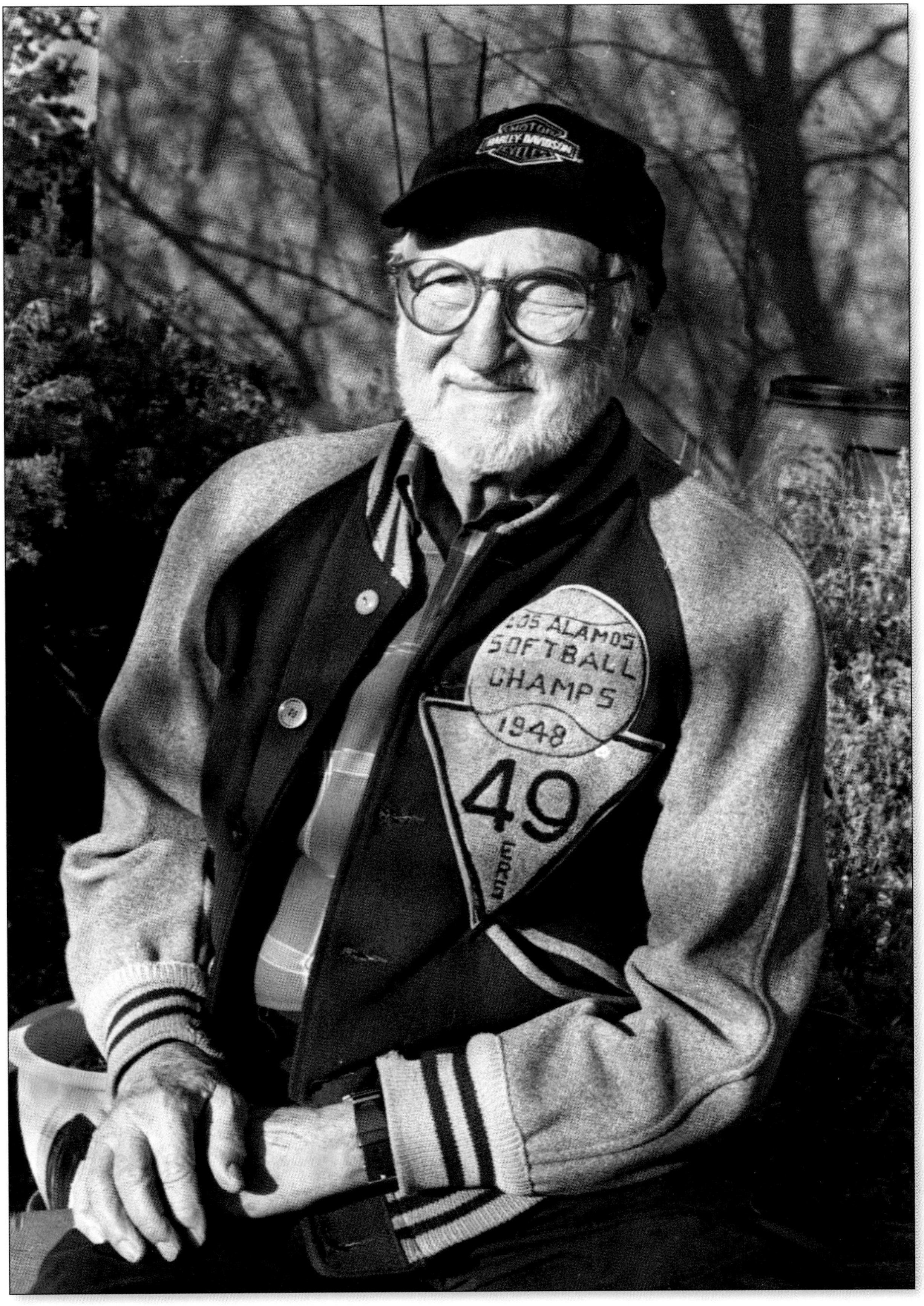
HARLEY-DAVIDSON
LOS ALAMOS
SOFTBALL
CHAMPS
1948
49

Harry Snowden, U.S. Army

✦ (SED) Special Engineer Detachment, May, 1944–1946
✦ Civilian employee 1946–1977
✦ Machinist in Physics Division—Worked on the cyclotron

Recreation was not in abundance at Los Alamos. Some of the available favorite pastimes were hiking the mountains; horseback riding (if you could get one of the MPs horses), and in the winter, skiing on the mountain slopes.

Harry Snowden provided the transportation for many of the skiers. On Sundays, said Snowden, he borrowed one of the government's six-by-six trucks. He loaded it with willing and exuberant people from The Hill who looked forward to a day of skiing on Sawyer's Hill.

Not all of the creativity took place *just* at the Lab: John Rogers and Snowden invented and built an ingenious rope tow with a handhold gripper for the skiers. The two men used tree hooks to climb a large tree where they mounted car wheels with big screws, and the rope was wound around the car wheels. A battery started the engine of an old Plymouth which powered the tow line which in turn towed the standing skier up the hill. The skier would hold onto the gripper and be pulled to the top of Sawyer's Hill.

Before the tow line was in operation on any particular Sunday, Harry or John had to carry the car battery and gasoline necessary to start the engine up the mountain. Often someone had to go down the mountain to get more gasoline, depending on the number of people using the lift.

"Sometimes the tow rope would break, and I had to splice it before the line could be in operation again." (Not as slick as a ski lift but better than trudging up the mountain without it.)

Among the skiers who took advantage of the truck ride as well as the ski tow line were Enrico Fermi and Niels Bohr, two of the top civilian scientists at Los Alamos. Everyone needed some relaxation and relief from the stress of the arduous and consuming task of developing the first atomic bomb. ✦

(Courtesy of Los Alamos Historical Society Archives)

SED Victor Kumin on ski run
(Courtesy of Los Alamos Historical Society Archives)

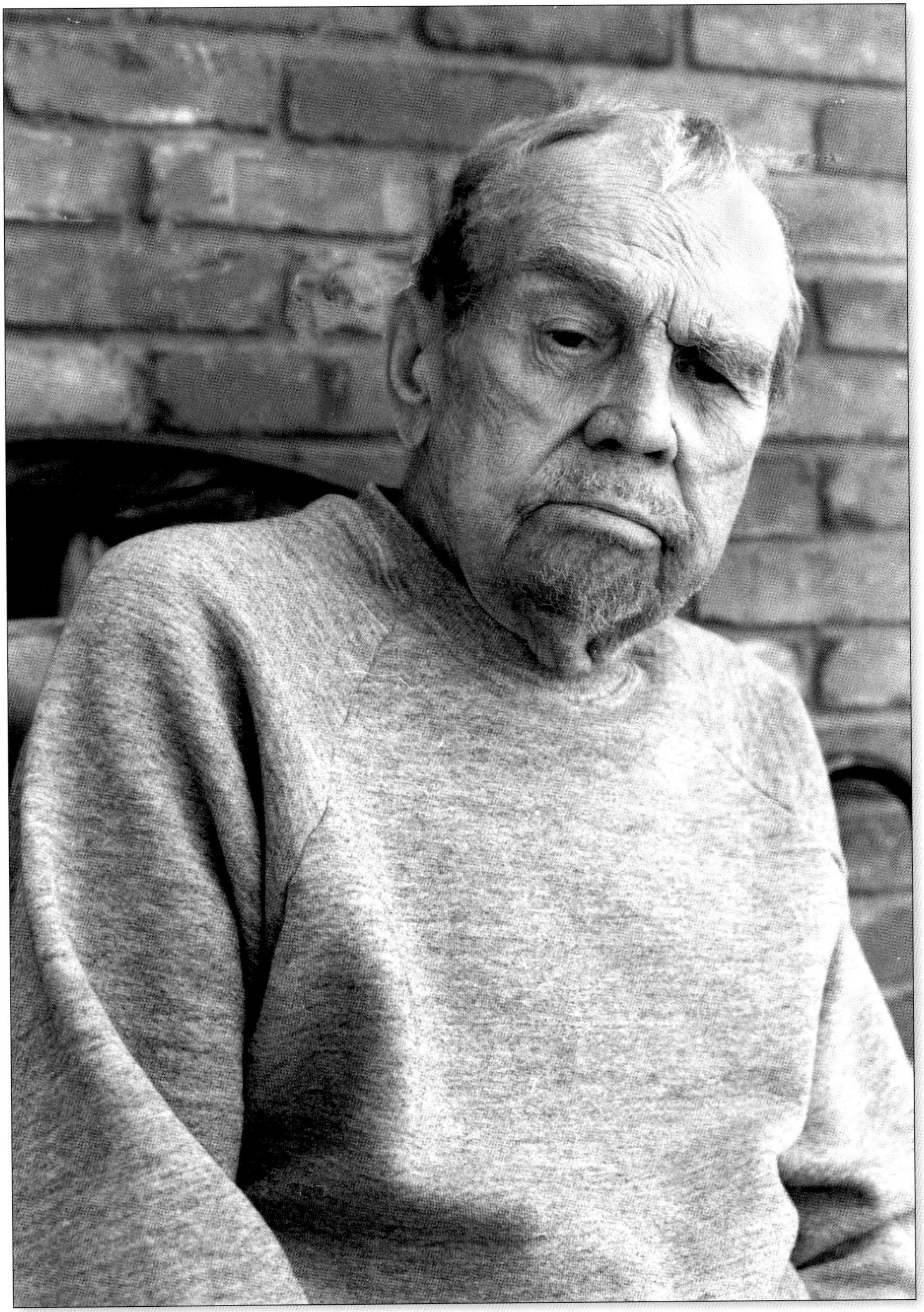

Vera Katherine "Katie" Stack

✦ Wife of Mechanical Engineer Francis Stack
✦ Secretary to Max Roy in administration, Worked March, 1944–1949

Katie Stack moved from Detroit to The Hill with her husband who was drafted into the Project by Fermi, Oppenheimer, and Bethe. Francis Stack designed the casings for "Fat Boy" and "Little Boy," the atomic bombs dropped on Japan. Katie became secretary to Max Roy.

"There was not much to do in Los Alamos, and one of our social activities was to go square dancing with the Native Americans from San Ildefonso Pueblo. Among the Native American dancers were the famous potters Maria Martinez and her husband Julian," Stack said. "Many of the Indians brought their babies in papoose carriers and just hung them on the backs of chairs," she continued.

At work, said Katie, no one got mail under their real names. This made it difficult for her to deliver the letters. There were no nameplates on the desks either. Max Roy, her boss, ended up delivering letters. "Every letter I wrote had to have five signatures, and I never knew to whom the letters went—because of the secrecy. In Detroit, I knew what I had to do at work. Here I had to continuously ask what Roy wanted me to do. It was all pretty confusing."

Stack loved to tell of some of the interesting happenings to the famous people who worked at the Lab. "Fermi often became so engrossed in his thoughts that he would walk into a telephone pole. In the cafeteria, Oppenheimer usually forgot his hat and lost it; this was a continuing saga."

"Fermi loved pastrami sandwiches. When his wife went back to Italy to visit after the war, she had to make him lots and lots of sandwiches before he would let her leave. She bought loaves and loaves of bread. This confused the other wives who had no idea what all the bread was for."

In 1956 the Stacks moved to Santa Fe because of the secrecy on The Hill. "When we went to parties no one could talk about the work in the Lab. At least in Santa Fe, you could hear what other people did at work even if you couldn't talk about what you did." ✦

Katie Stack and husband Francis Stack

Max Roy

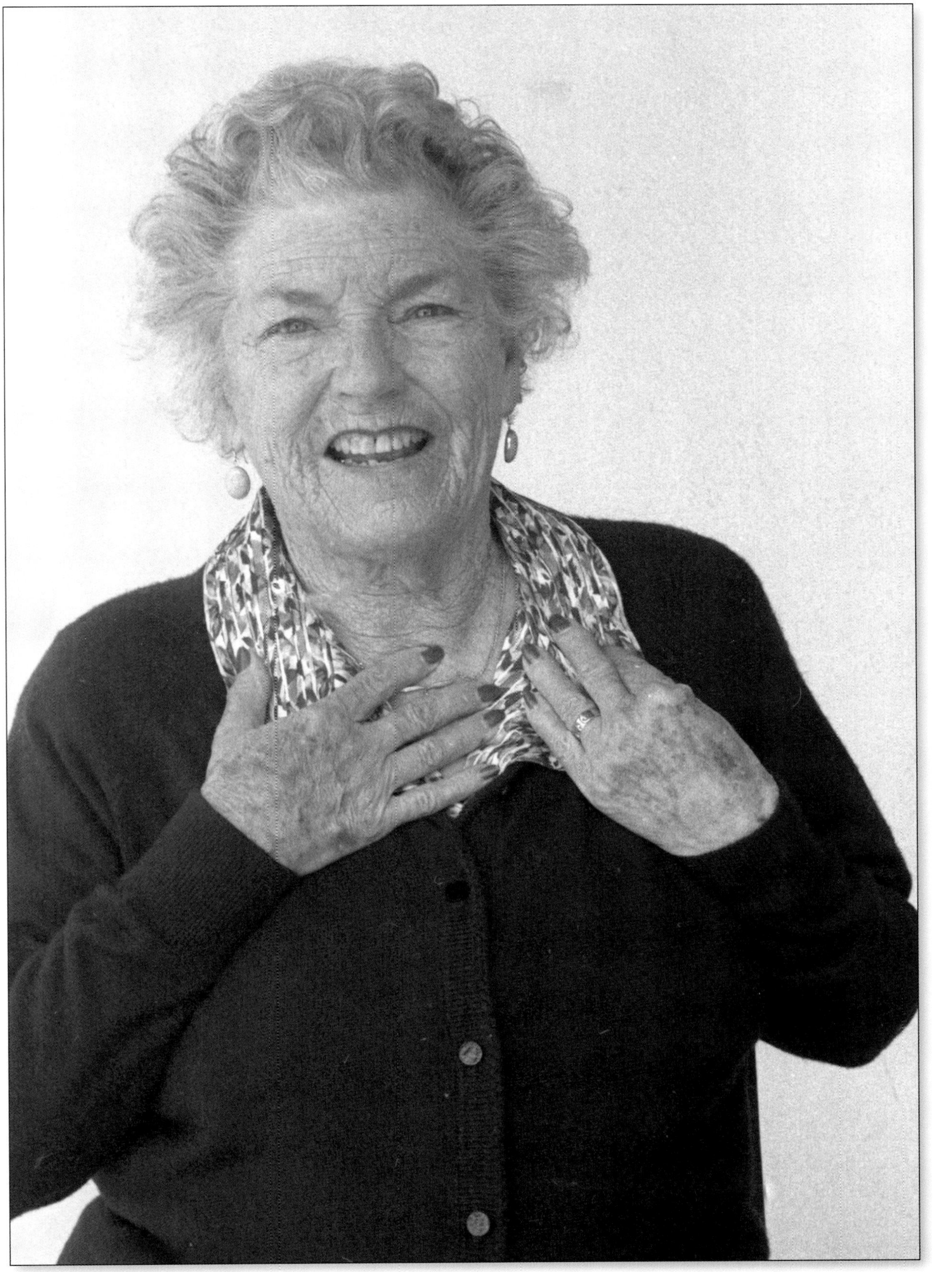

Rudolph "Rudy" O. Velasco, U.S. Army

- ✦ (SED) Special Engineer Detachment, worked at Oak Ridge, Tenn. Lab, 1944–1945
- ✦ Worked at Los Alamos 1945–1946
- ✦ Civilian employee 1946–1950, 1984–1996
- ✦ Nuclear engineer, Chemistry/Metallurgy Division
- ✦ Performed nickel plating of plutonium hemispheres

Soon after Rudy Velasco arrived at Los Alamos, he met Callie Maass, a young chemist from a ranching family in South Dakota. She was an accomplished horsewoman and had won many barrel racing competitions in high school rodeos. Velasco, smitten from the moment they met, would go to any length to impress Maass. In fact, he bought a horse, sight unseen, from Paul McKenzie. McKenzie brought the horse and a less-than-perfect used Western saddle to The Hill from his home in Oklahoma for Velasco.

Velasco was somewhat experienced in riding horses; at the University of Arizona he was a member of the Cavalry ROTC. He was gung-ho about going riding with Maass. One small detail he had overlooked: the better army saddles had forward-mounted stirrups which required posting when the horse was trotting—western saddles had stirrups which hung from the middle which did not require posting

On subsequent rides with Callie, the couple was an interesting contrast. Callie sat her horse, a Morgan mare, beautifully, but, Rudy sat his horse with his legs stuck out from the sides of the horse; he could not get used to the different stirrup arrangement. To make matters worse, Rudy's horse was a stubborn, Roman-nosed gelding. "Riding was a butt-bouncing experience; my teeth chattered when I tried to trot," reported Velasco.

As if that wasn't bad enough, Velasco said wryly, a CMR division leader, Dr. Eric Jette, saw the couple riding one afternoon and, being himself an avid horseman, complimented Callie on her fine horse and saddle and the graceful way she rode.

"Jette looked at me; he looked at my horse; he looked at my saddle; he looked at my legs sticking out. He said absolutely nothing. Silence, more eloquent than words, expressed his opinion."

There is a happy ending to this story. Callie Maass, not to be deterred by Rudy's mere lack of horsemanship, saw the true worth of the young man who went to great lengths to win her affection. The young couple married and reared seven children in Los Alamos. ✦

Callie Maass and her horse

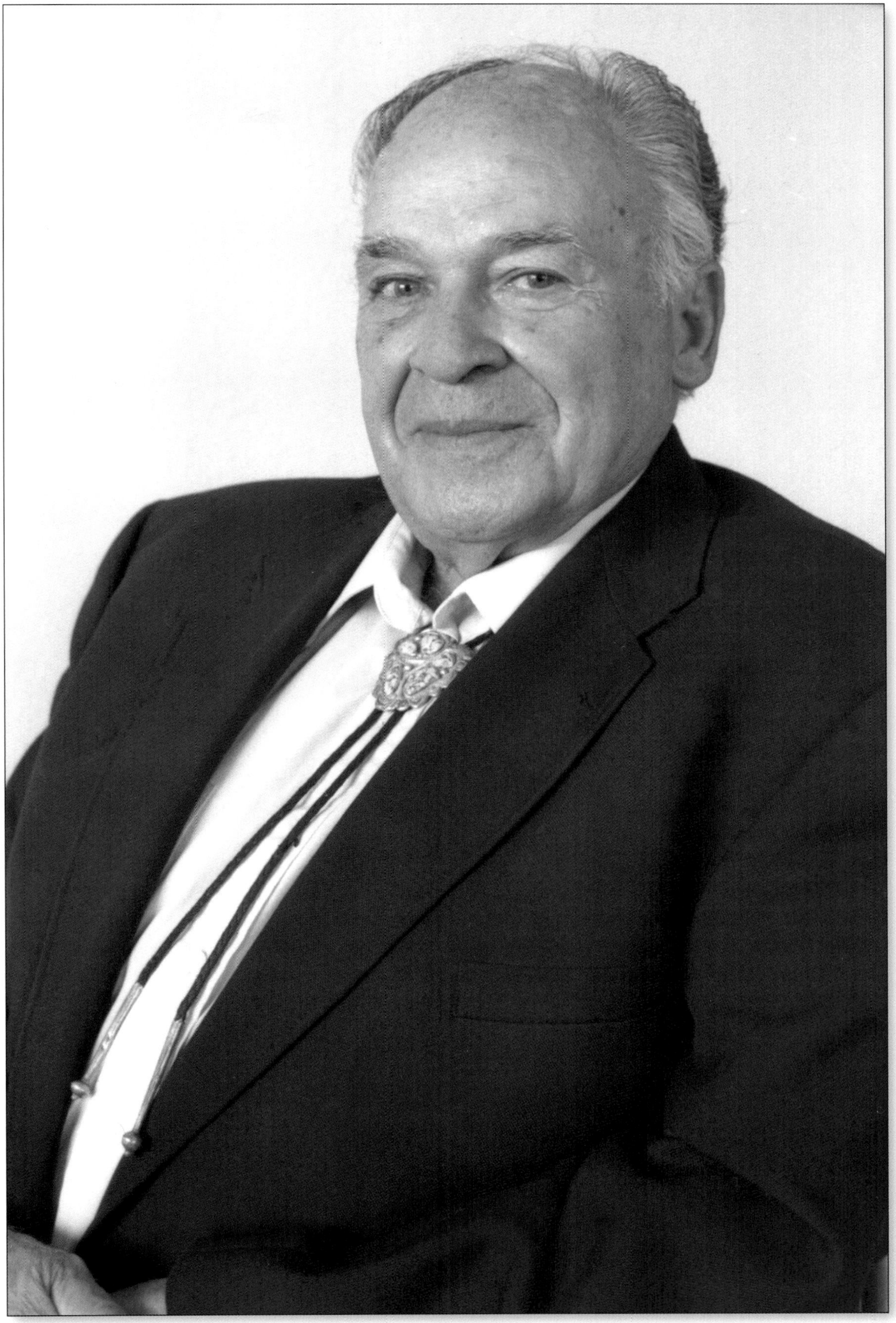

Robert "Bob" Walker, civilian

- Physicist, worked 1943–1945
- Involved with calibration of radium beryllium
- Absolute calibration of neutron source and Calibrations at Trinity Test Site

Bob Walker came to Los Alamos from the Metallurgical Lab at the University of Chicago. He was sent with a special package which, he said, made him very important. This was to be his "day in the sun," so to speak. In fact, he was so important at that time that he didn't have to check in with Dorothy McKibbin in Santa Fe. He was to be taken straight to The Hill with no in-between stops.

In his pocket was a tiny sample of plutonium to be delivered to the scientists on The Hill. A G.I. driver was to pick up Walker at the airport. The driver didn't recognize him at first, just walked right past him. So much for being "Mr. Important," noted Walker.

"The soldier did not like the posting," Walker said. "He was told he was guarding something, but he didn't know what it was and didn't like that."

"You must be very important," the G.I. told him. "Oppie said that if anyone suspicious-looking comes up to the car, just shoot him."

(Courtesy of Los Alamos National Lab Archives)

"I guess that was to be my claim to fame, and it was short-lived," reported Walker. "Once I gave up the glass vial containing the plutonium, I ceased to be important."

Nevertheless, Walker went on to perform important work, especially on July 16, 1945, at Trinity Site, where the first atomic bomb test took place. As he told it, "The entire physics department did the measurements of the air blast, the intensity, the yield of the device, and the ground measurements. I installed the Piezo electric gauges."

Walker watched the test from a bunker six miles from the blast. "There was a huge ball of fire, like nothing I had ever seen before," he exclaimed.

"I didn't have a big negative reaction about the dropping of the atomic bombs on Hiroshima and Nagasaki. They were going to end the war, and I could get back to the business of going to school."

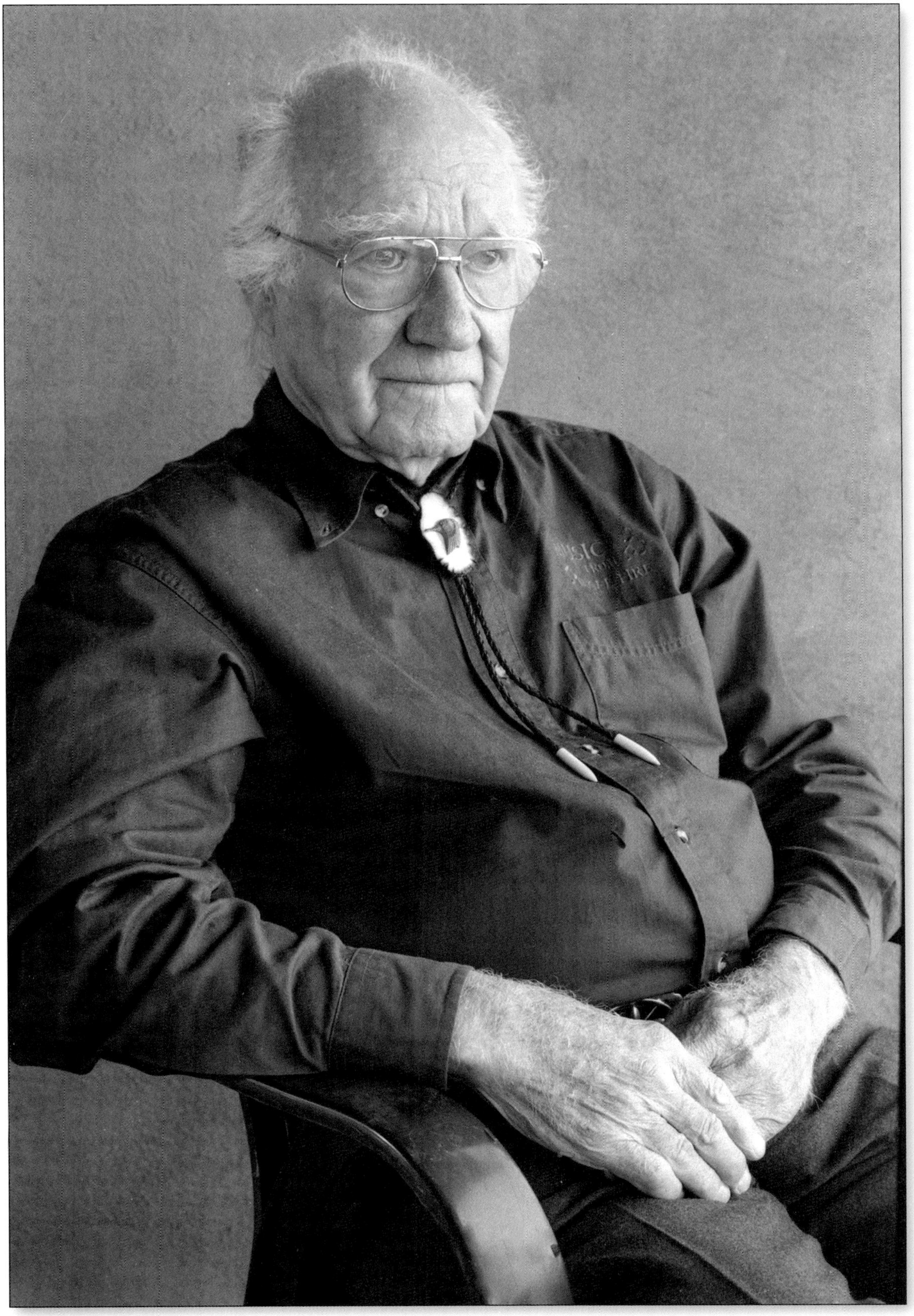

Jacob J. "Jay" Wechsler, U.S. Army

- ✦ (SED) Special Engineer Detachment, 1944–1946
- ✦ Civilian employee 1946–1982
- ✦ Engineer and physicist
- ✦ Physics Division, weapons development, Explosive and hydrodynamic testing

---

Jay Wechsler had a strong interest in music and played the trombone in a band on The Hill. The band played at many Saturday night dances. One night at a dance, a stranger approached Wechsler and the band's trumpeter, Don Lovelace, and asked the two to play in his band. This man was Gus Bustos.

Wechsler and Lovelace agreed to play with the Bustos band. Gus Bustos took his popular music group to play all around the area—in Ojo Caliente, Peña Blanca, Pojaque, Española, and Santa Fe.

Bustos told Wechsler and Lovelace that the audience was mostly Spanish and sometimes, if the drinking got serious, altercations could erupt and it might get pretty rough. Because Wechsler and Lovelace were white, they might get the brunt of a fight. "If I say, 'Let's play *The Blue Danube Waltz*,' you fellas get the hell out."

One night, sure enough, the drinking looked as if it would get out of hand. In a quiet, controlled voice, Bustos said, "Fellas, let's play *The Blue Danube Waltz*." Lovelace and Wechsler hurriedly put their instruments away and headed for the exit. They hopped into Wechsler's La Salle automobile and zoomed away.

Wechsler recalled riding the MPs' horses some Sunday mornings. He really looked forward to these outings. One Sunday he went alone to borrow a horse for an early morning ride on the mountain trails. The MPs picked out a horse for him which he subsequently saddled and bridled. He had hardly gotten into the saddle when the horse snorted and took off at a gallop heading down what is now Trinity Drive. Away they went just like the Lone Ranger. "I don't know how I managed to stay on, but the horse finally slowed down and trotted back to the stable," laughed Wechsler. "This was not a horse to take on the trails." The MPs had knowingly given Wechsler a horse that would run if there were no other horses to accompany it. The MPs surely had a good laugh.

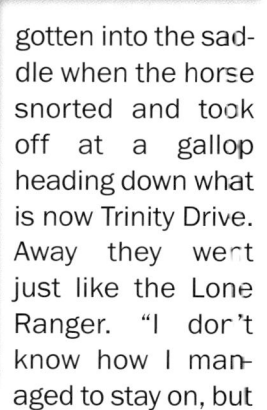

Wechsler was the first coach of the Los Alamos Girls Swim Team. He was a longtime member of the Los Alamos Ski Club and was a ski instructor. In addition to these activities, he had been a leader in numerous civic organizations, serving on many of their boards. ✦

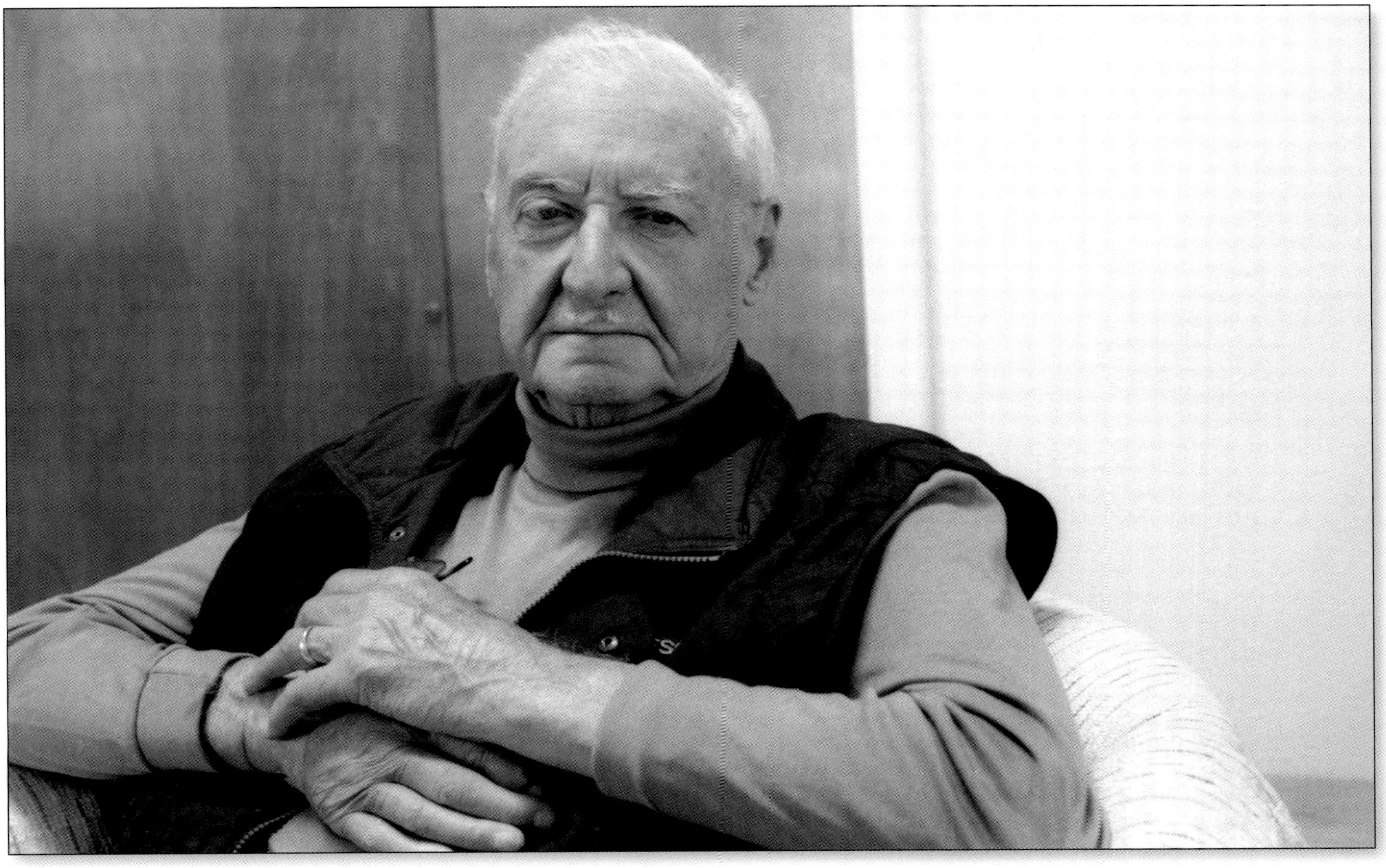

Dulcinea "Duddy" Wilder

- ✦ Wife of Chemical Engineer Ed Wilder
- ✦ Lived at Los Alamos from early June, 1945—1970

(Duddy Wilder's husband Ed was a navy man, and a chemical engineeer assigned to Los Alamos for the war. She notes that he was never on a ship until he got out of the navy.)

Doing the laundry on The Hill was a social occasion. Everyone had a child's wagon, Duddy Wilder remembered, and the women hauled their dirty clothes to the laundry in their wagons. It was a self-service laundry with clotheslines in back. "Nobody had a washing machine at that time," Wilder went on, "and we had a lot of laundry to wash because most people had children." Later, the only way to get one's own washer was to have a baby. (It was rumored that some people may have had a baby for just that reason.)

The laundry had four or five washers, Wilder related, and the washers had wringers. The woman who ran the laundry would use a mangle to iron your clothes—if you wanted that, Wilder said.

Behind the laundry there was a playground for the children where Wilder remembered her daughter Ellen on a seesaw.

The laundry was a meeting place. It was also a way to forge friendships, to meet newcomers as well as friends.

Wilder recalled that she and Pearl Norwood, a close friend, gave each other hair "permanents." Companionship saved the wives from abject loneliness because their husbands worked such long hours. The laundry took the place of a "kaffeeklatsch" for many Los Alamos women during the war years. ✦

Duddy Wilder and family shortly after World War II

137

Alfred "Al" Zeltmann, U.S. Army

+ **(SED) Special Engineer Detachment, 1944–1946**
+ **Worked as civilian 1946–1984**
+ **Physical chemist**
+ **Did chemical counts of neutrons**

Al Zeltmann was at Los Alamos, but his wife had to remain in New York because wives of servicemen were not allowed on The Hill. When Zeltmann received letters from his wife, she would often complain that he did not express any affection in his letters—this upset her terribly especially since they had to live so far from each other. All outgoing and incoming mail had to go through the censors; there were no secrets from the censors who, of course, read everyone's mail. One day Zeltmann received another letter from his wife, again complaining that she received letters devoid of affection for her. The censors must have tired of reading her laments; at the bottom of the letter, the censor had written a curt bit of advice: "Tell her what she wants to know."

Some young civilians at the Lab were working with Zeltmann. One of them took every opportunity to goof off and not pay attention to his assigned job. In other words, he was a slacker. When Zeltmann mentioned the civilian's poor attitude, one of the supervisors responded, "Well, you have to make allowances; he's unhappy because he wants to go back to school."

"I thought that was ironic because many of us servicemen *also* wanted to go back to school for advanced degrees—but first we had to complete an important job at Los Alamos," commented Zeltmann wryly.

Many of the people on The Hill had horses. Zeltmann recalls that John Rodriguez, a civilian who came to Los Alamos from Brown University, not only had a horse but also a burro. The two animals were kept together in a barn located in Omega Canyon. Now this was not your ordinary run-of-the-mill burro; this was a sensitive burro. The burro didn't like to poop in the barn which was his home. Not only that, but he didn't like the horse pooping in the barn either. He taught the horse to do his "business" outside instead. "As I said, not your average burro," emphasized Zeltmann.

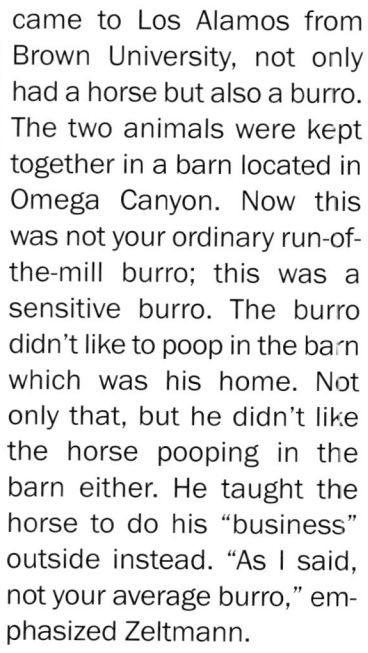

"Unfortunately, John Rodriguez was the first person to die from beryllium poisoning. He was exposed to vapors from the substance," related Zeltmann. "Rodriguez had worked with beryllium at Brown University before continuing his work at Los Alamos and had been married only a short time. The Lab gave the family a meager $15,000 death benefit, and Rodriguez's wife and brother were trying to decide how to divide it." A sad commentary on a sad story... ✦

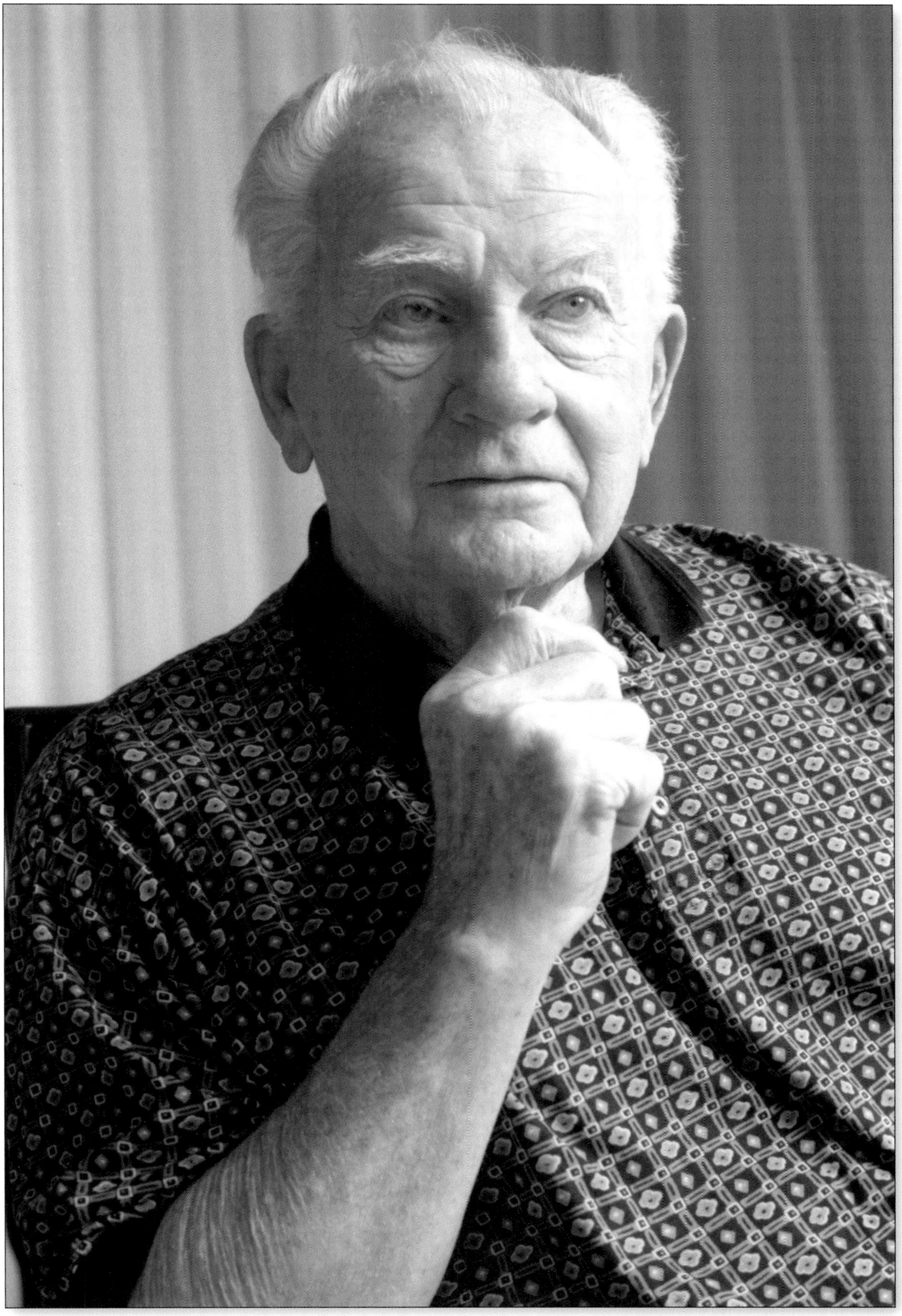

About the Author

Author and photographer aj Melnick moved to Santa Fe, New Mexico, in 1994 from Dallas, Texas, where she began developing her photographic skills some three decades ago. In New Mexico she has continued her photography studies with Siegfried Halus, Norman Mauskopf, Andre Ruesch, and Miguel Gandert. Her work has been exhibited in galleries and museums, in juried group shows, and in individual shows. She holds a bachelor's degree in journalism from The University of Texas, and a master's degree in counseling from North Texas State University. Melnick is listed in the following *Marquis Who's Who* biographical volumes; *Who's Who of American Women*, *Who's Who of the West*, *Who's Who of the World*, and *Who's Who of America*. She lives with her husband Harold and rescued German Shepherd, Kolbe, at The Montecito in Santa Fe, New Mexico. ✦